LETTERS FROM A SOVIET PRISON CAMP

Letters
From a
Soviet
Prison Camp

Mikhail Khorev

MONARCH PUBLICATIONS

Eastbourne

Published under licence from Missionswerk Friedensstimme, Gummersbach, West Germany.

Copyright © 1986 Missionswerk Friedenstimme, Gummersbach, West Germany.
Copyright © 1988 (English edition) Friedensstimme (UK), (Voice of Peace), PO Box 10, Leicester, LE3 2FX England (Registered Charity No. 326879)

First published in UK 1988

Front cover design by Vic Mitchell

British Library cataloguing in Publication Data

Khorev, Mikhail, *1931–*
Letters from a Soviet prison camp.
1. Soviet Union. christian prisoners.
Khorev, Mikhail, 1931–
I. Title
365'.45'0924

ISBN 1-85424-096-X
0-86760-068-3 (Albatross)
0-9513543-0-2 (Radstock Press Ltd)

Production and printing in Great Britain for
MONARCH PUBLICATIONS LTD
Lottbridge Drove, Eastbourne, E Sussex BN23 6NT by
Nuprint Ltd, Station Road, Harpenden, Herts AL5 4SE.

Contents

Preface

Whenever I think about friends and fellow believers who have suffered some of the worst punishment in prisons and penal camps for Christ's sake, I think above all of Mikhail Ivanovich Khorev. He is known fervently and simply as Brother Misha by his friends, relations and by other believers of the awakened fellowship of Evangelical Christian Baptists in the USSR.

Mikhail Ivanovich is a great friend of children and of Christian youth, a gifted and passionate preacher as well as an indefatigable and dynamic servant of the Christian church.

He was born on 19th December 1931 in Leningrad where he grew up and later became a Christian. Early in life he lost his father who was arrested in 1937 for his active service as an evangelist and who never returned home.

From the start Mikhail Ivanovich played an active role in the 'initiative group' which was to unite many Christians in the USSR and lead them to inner freedom — but at the cost of much suffering and tears. Mikhail Ivanovich himself was not spared any of this and at the present time he is serving his fourth term of imprisonment. Between terms of imprisonment he served the churches as an evangelist. In the course of this work he visited a great number of churches. During his trial in

1966 the judge ordered him to name the towns where he had preached. Mikhail Ivanovich replied, very calmly and very frankly, 'It is very difficult for me to do that. It would be a lot easier for me to name the towns where I have not preached.'

Mikhail Ivanovich and I were arrested together in 1966. On 16th May of that year around 500 believers from 140 localities in the Soviet Union had travelled to Moscow because of increasing persecution, in the hope of presenting a report to the authorities about the situation of believers in the country. After two days of fruitless waiting around outside the doors of the Central Committee of the Communist Party of the Soviet Union, the delegates were arrested. This took place on 17th May.

On 19th May Mikhail Ivanovich and I were commissoned by leading brethren to go to the same Central Committee building to speak on behalf of these arrested delegates. As we approached the Central Committee building I said to Mikhail Ivanovich, 'Dear brother, see what a wonderful morning it is, so clear and bright! The sun's shining and the air has that fresh spring-like quality about it—but perhaps in an hour from now we will both be sitting in a dim cell and breathing foul air. It is still not too late for us to change our minds. Perhaps it would be better if I went on alone.'

Mikhail Ivanovich smiled gently and replied, 'Brother, what on earth are you on about? We can't leave our brothers in distress. Don't you remember the thirteenth verse of John 15 where it says, "Greater love hath no man than this, that he lay down his life for his friends".' And then he added, 'We will go together and say, "Release our brothers and sisters and keep us instead!" '

We shook hands and went to the reception building of the Central Committee. There we handed to the officials our identity cards as well as the petition from the leadership of our association requesting the release of the 500 delegates.

An hour later the head of the reception centre of the Central Committee met us and talked with us for half an hour or so about the situation of Christians in the USSR and about the fate of the delegates. After leaving the reception building we were set about, there on the street, in broad daylight, by about ten KGB officials.[1] Within a short space of time they had our arms pinned behind our backs and we were dragged off. As they pushed me into one waiting car I just caught sight of Mikhail Ivanovich being thrown into another.

It was not until after my release three years later that we met again. Mikhail Ivanovich had received a sentence that was half a year shorter than mine. So he was already fully au fait with the situation of the Christian churches in the country, and came to tell me about it.

'Well, Mikhail Ivanovich, aren't you sorry that we went to the Central Committee to enquire about the fate of the delegates?' I asked him.

'Of course not!' he replied. 'That was a very necessary step in the cause of defending God's kingdom in our country. Anyway, I have to admit to you that prison is a very useful school for our education and for the testing of the genuineness of our faith.' Then he added, 'I'm grateful to the Lord for this school and for his leading.'

On 28th January 1980 Mikhail Ivanovich returned to this school. It was there that he wrote these letters to his sons. They were published in the newspaper of the unregistered Evangelical Christian Baptists, *Vestnik Istiny* ('The Messenger of Truth'), and were a primary cause of his being resentenced in December 1984 to a further two years' imprisonment, just one month prior to the completion of his earlier sentence.

On 19th December, 1986, Mikhail Ivanovich Khorev was released from imprisonment. On the next day, 20th

December, a worship service was held in Kishinev to welcome him home. Around a thousand believers gathered to meet Mikhail Ivanovich. Many had travelled from other parts of the country just to be present at this service. After many years of bonds and separation from his friends and family, Mikhail Ivanovich once again preached about Jesus Christ. Thus, from the first days of freedom, Pastor Khorev has taken an active role in the ministry of the persecuted church.

Fifteen years have now passed since I last saw brother Khorev. Although he has been free now for some time, we have never even been able to talk by telephone. In August of 1987, I was in West Germany, and wanted very much to contact him, if only to hear my dear friend's voice for five minutes. But all my attempts at contact were without results.

Then on 23rd April, 1988, here in America, I unexpectedly received a call from the Soviet Union, from Kiev. 'Georgi! Greetings in the name of our Lord Jesus Christ!' It was the voice of Mikhail Ivanovich. 'Greetings to you from all of the brothers and sisters here, and especially from brother Gennadi Kryuchkov!'

Praise the Lord for this wonderful opportunity to hear the voice of this dear brother in the faith. And more than this, to hear his joy and hope in the Lord!

Dear reader, I pray that brother Khorev's testimony of faith, suffering, and God's blessing will stir your soul to love Jesus Christ even more, to cherish your Bible, and to pray for a spiritual awakening in your land!

GEORGI P VINS[2]
International Representative of the
Council of (Unregistered) Evangelical Christian
Baptists in the USSR, Elkhart, USA.

The Fifteenth Day

On 19th May 1966, I was arrested together with Georgi Petrovich Vins and taken to Lefortovo prison. Everything was exactly as I had imagined it. From the first day of the investigation I was told that they wished to free me. Every day I was taken for interrogation and was asked how and by whom had the delegation to Moscow been organised and what part had I played in it? I told them at length of my conversion to the Lord, whom I now serve with all my strength, all my dedication and all my love.

Every day they would say to me, 'But you are not the person in charge. Why do you take this responsibility upon yourself? Simply confess that you took no part in the delegation. Admit that you were only there by chance and then you can go home in peace.'

I refused to say such a thing, but neither did I admit that I was an active participant. All of this was an internal affair of the Christian church.

The fourteenth day of my imprisonment in Lefortovo remains especially imprinted on my memory. In the morning I was called for interrogation. The interrogator, who was normally very active and had a lot to say, was sitting this time in the furthest corner of the little room and a civilian, aged about fifty, spoke instead. From his demeanour it was easy to see that he was of superior rank to the interrogator.

He turned to me. 'Mikhail Ivanovich, today your fate will be decided. We want to free you to go home. But just tell me what will you do when you get home?'

To gain time I said, 'I don't understand your question at all, could you repeat it please?' As he repeated it I prayed silently, 'Lord, what shall I answer?'

Suddenly there I was standing at the threshold of freedom. Anyone who has ever been under arrest knows how intensely you long for it. You close your eyes and imagine the door opening. You live for freedom.

But now I had to answer the question 'What will you do?'

I knew what they wanted me to say: 'Why do you ask? I have a wife, small children, enough to worry about at home.' This answer would immediately have opened the doors of the prison.

With a desperate effort at self-composure I replied, 'You ask what I will do. Don't you know that I am an evangelist in the Council of Christian Churches? I was called to this service and have now been separated from my work for fourteen days. My whole calendar has been upset. I should now be in the Urals, Siberia and Asia. So I will have to make up for lost time.'

The superior fixed his eyes on me. 'Mikhail Ivanovich, you are deliberately making this conversation difficult. Give me a precise answer. Do you want to go home?'

'Yes, of course I do.'

'Well then, the prison doors will open for you today, but they will not be opened by an angel like they were for Peter, or so the Bible says, but by the prison warder. We will sign a document which states that you will be released and we will put the official seal on it.'

I said, 'Then I simply do not understand why you have kept me here imprisoned for fourteen days if the doors can be opened so easily.'

'Don't you worry about it. We shall simply stamp the documents to say that you were sentenced to fifteen days' imprisonment. You will go home and lead a peaceful life.'

He saw that I was shaking my head. He said, 'Why do you want to travel around all over the country? You have small children, your wife is often sick. Go home and spend time with your family. You're a pastor, good. We can understand that. OK, carry on your service in the Church of Kishinev, or better still, carry out your work in the Republic of Moldavia. Haven't you got enough to do there? But no, you want a general's epaulettes!'

The midday break was approaching and I was taken back to my cell. I knew that I would be recalled during the afternoon, so I fell down on my knees and prayed to the Lord.

What was God's will? Two feelings were struggling against each other inside me: 'Don't give way', and 'Why make things more difficult? Let everything work out as it will. The main thing is to keep quiet at the proper time.'

I asked my Lord, 'Lord, help me not to make any mistakes.'

I was called back that afternoon.

'What decision have you made?'

'Excuse me, but I don't need to make a decision. I already made my decision when I promised to serve the Lord. You, however, have got a decision to make.'

'Now just be careful. If we sentence you now, then it will be a lot easier to give you a further sentence in the future. It is not easy to go to prison the first time, but later on every time you commit an offence you will be sentenced for it. Just think about that.'

I replied, 'I am not asking you to either keep me here or to release me. I am saying that it is unjust of you to deprive me of my freedom. If you release me now, you will be a criminal because you detained me when I was not guilty. If, however, you condemn me then you will be guilty of an even greater crime because you condemn me when I am innocent.'

'Fine, now I understand,' remarked the superior. 'He really wants to stay in prison. OK! The fifteen days are up tomorrow, and as soon as the final day is past you will be resentenced, and we will find a good reason for doing that. So make your mind up, and let us know when you have.'

The morning of the fifteenth day broke. My morale had really sunk low. For almost the entire night I had not been able to sleep, lying awake thinking that the decision lay in my hands. Freedom or imprisonment: which should I choose?

As usual I was awakened at six o'clock and given breakfast. I declined to eat and fasted again. My neighbour asked me, 'What is bothering you so much?'

I explained everything to him.

'If I had the honour of standing in the dock for such a reason,' he said, 'then this cell bunk would be a thousand times more preferable to me than making any compromise.'

'What would you advise then?' I asked.

'What would I advise? Well, I noticed that during the night you got up to pray, and that yesterday, and today again, you have been unsettled. Well, if it's in your heart to knock on the doors, why don't you turn to your highest authority, and not to me? Pray to God, and do what he tells you.'

This advice pleased me. I was happy and comforted. Several times I went down on my knees, and after praying the thought of knocking on the door and asking for a discussion did not come to me again.

And so the fifteenth day passed, one of the most important days of my life—*a day of triumph*.

Part One

The Trial

Proceedings Instituted

On 23rd May 1980 Vera Khoreva, Mikhail's wife, was summoned to the office of the Prosecutor of the Soviet Republic of Moldavia. Here she was threatened by Mr Zurkan, the interrogator for especially serious crimes, and by one of his colleagues from the KGB, Mr Tokarev, with prosecution for slander if she should send a petition to the government or if she should inform her friends about the date of proceedings against Khorev. They promised at the end of the conversation that she would be informed of the date of the trial the day before, and that all the relatives of the accused would be allowed to attend.

On 26th May Vera Khoreva was still waiting at home for news. When by 11.15 am no news had come, she went to the Supreme Court of the Moldavian Soviet Socialist Republic (MSSR) to enquire about the date. It was here that she was informed that the proceedings against her husband had already been in progress since early that morning, on the premises of the tinned food factory in Kishinev.

Vera Khoreva immediately informed several relatives and eventually they reached the factory at 1 pm. Approximately sixty auxiliary police, twenty policemen and twenty plain-clothes policemen were standing outside the building.

At first, only a few of Khorev's relatives turned up. Only after pleading for a long time were they and a few friends, about 20 people altogether, allowed into the courtroom, with seating capacity for approximately 120. (The majority of places were occupied by factory activists and other functionaries. Any relatives of the accused who arrived later were not allowed inside.)

Many of Khorev's friends waited outside the courtroom for the afternoon of the first and for the whole of the second day of the trial. All they wanted was to see Mikhail Ivanovich for just a few minutes, but their wishes were not granted.

The proceedings against Mikhail Ivanovich Khorev, member of the Council of Christian Churches, took place on 26th and 27th May 1980 before the Supreme Court of the Moldavian Soviet Socialist Republic. Khorev was assigned a defence lawyer even though he had declined having one.

The Afternoon of 26th May

Judge: Would the accused please address the court?

Khorev: With regard to the events that took place on 2nd May 1978, please note that only witnesses from the police and from the authorities have been called. For the most part their testimony has been pure fabrication. The most serious charge brought against me has been that I incited young men of military age to refuse national service. In my defence I request firstly to summon the following witnesses: L I Yevdoshenko, I R Shepuryenko,

P D Posiorko. Then, with regard to the charge of having conducted a marriage ceremony in the village of Chuchelyeny, since again only witnesses from one side have been called, for example, the chairman of the village soviet and his secretary, I would like to summon the following witnesses who were present at this wedding ceremony: M I Prutyanu, V G Khoreva and S G Apostu.

The judge consulted with the prosecutor and after a brief exchange it was announced that Khorev's requests would not, for the moment, be granted. At the close of the session the judge declared that Khorev's requests had been declined.

Khorev stood up.

Judge: Do you plead guilty?

Khorev: No.

Judge: Are you ready to state your case?

Khorev: Yes.

Public Prosecutor: I agree to cross-examine Khorev first and then the witnesses in the order stated in the indictment.

Judge: What do you answer to the indictment?

Khorev: There are eight points to the indictment:

1. The youth meeting on 1st and 2nd May 1976;
2. The youth meeting on 1st and 2nd May 1977;
3. The youth meeting on 1st and 2nd May 1978;
4. The marriage ceremony of M A Prutyanu in the village of Chuchelyeny;
5. The meeting in the city of Kishinev;
6. The visit of friends to the Kroeker's home in the city of Bendery;
7. The visit of friends to the Azarov's home in the city of Leningrad;
8. The visit of friends to the village of Sofiyevka.

The three youth meetings were the usual ones held during the Mayday holidays. If I am being charged with having organised these meetings, then I have to admit that I count it an honour, even though I was not the only one responsible.

We met in a quiet, remote place in order not to disturb anyone. Since I was an active participant myself in these meetings I find the accusation brought against us totally absurd in this respect. As we left the meeting place, we noticed lively groups of five, ten or perhaps fifteen people enjoying themselves and listening to music on a tape recorder. They were not disturbed by us. Didn't our 300 young people also have the same rights as these other citizens? Didn't they have the same right to enjoy themselves? None of us made any smutty speeches, but we were only singing and praising God. If this is why I am being threatened with three years' imprisonment, then this charge is totally groundless. No one can reproach us for breaking down trees or leaving litter around, nor did we disturb anyone's peace. Had there been the remotest likelihood of our annoying anybody there we would have moved further away.

Judge: Were there children present? Did they sing and take part?

Khorev: Yes, there were children present.

Judge: Were any of these children of preschool age? Did they sing too?

Khorev: I don't know who sang and who didn't sing.

Judge: Did you address young men of military age in your speech?

Khorev: A young man who had just been called up passed me a piece of paper asking me to pray for him. When I, he and several others had prayed, I suggested that we should sing. After that I said that the situation he was going into would be quite a different one than he was used to, and I exhorted all those soon to go into the army to be conscientious and faithful and not to forget to pray. Above all, I encouraged them to confess their Christian faith openly. But here I am being charged with inciting them to refuse to take the military oath. Each citizen has to make up his own mind about that military oath and it is not the church's business to interfere.

Judge: Now, what took place on 22nd August in the tent erected at 88 Post Street in Kishinev?

Khorev: It was a regular Christian service. Then police officers and plain-clothes men suddenly appeared and turned their cameras on me. I did not find anything incriminating about these photographs. I consider it quite normal that children were present because you find them present in any church. I don't dispute that I led the service, but neither do I see any offence in that. For me to communicate my convictions to others is not a crime but rather my sacred duty.

Judge: Did the officials not instruct you to discontinue the service and to disperse?

Khorev: We answered them that we were not on the street but were gathered inside someone's garden and were not obstructing anyone. Throughout the whole time they deliberately kept the camera pointed at me. After the service we talked with the police officers.

Judge: What took place on 18th September 1978 in the village of Chuchelyeny?

Khorev: That was a hard Sunday. The bridegroom, M A Prutyanu and his bride, R S Kyriak, both members of our church, had asked me to carry out the wedding ceremony. A tent had been erected for this purpose in the courtyard. About 400 friends had been invited. Unfortunately, the Friday prior to this, the village was placed under quarantine and no one was allowed access. These circumstances had been orchestrated by the KGB.

Judge: Are you informed fully of the statements of the witnesses?

Khorev: Yes.

Judge: In the court documentation no mention is made of the word 'quarantine'.

Khorev: Well, there's absolutely no way of contesting the fact that the police banned all entry on the grounds that the village was under quarantine. All the normal means of access had been closed, and so the only way open to us was to go through the vineyards. The bridal couple left Kishinev on Saturday at 6 pm. After many difficulties they reached the village sixty-five kilometres away on Sunday morning.

Judge: Are you addressing the charge?

Khorev: In the charge it speaks of 'under the pretence of holding a marriage ceremony'. But this was a legal wedding, and one which has been registered at the state registry office. A child has even been born of this marriage. So why then is there now suddenly a question that this was only a 'pretence marriage ceremony'? We are also charged with having used loud speakers. But these were all in the tent and were not brought out on to the street or fixed to trees.

Judge: You are charged with:

1. having sung too loudly;
2. having permitted the presence of children;
3. having preached too loudly;
4. having held a procession in the street.

Khorev: I'm afraid that the number of people present made the use of speakers absolutely indispensable. What's more, we were using several musical instruments which needed amplification through loud speakers. As to the presence of children, well, show me a wedding where children do not take part.

Judge: You are accused of having instructed those children in religion.

Khorev: Instruction takes place in schools.

Judge: But you are not registered.

Khorev: And we won't get registered either.

Judge: Why not?

Khorev: Because of the legislation concerning religious cults.[3]

Judge: Why don't you like this legislation?

Khorev: Allow me to speak about this question separately.

Letter to Leonid Brezhnev

To the Central Committee of the Communist Party of the Soviet Union, to L I Brezhnev, from M I Khorev, member of the Council of ECB Churches,[4] presently serving a five-year prison sentence in Omsk.

Leonid Ilich!   13.10.82.

After considerable reflection I have decided to write a letter to you in which I would like to share with you my thinking about the present situation.

I won't go into the reason for my arrest and imprisonment, since you already know that the only thing I'm guilty of is serving God. If I were to write to you in detail about the charges levelled against me, charges for which I am serving a five-year prison sentence, then that would be a whole letter in itself. But this letter has a different purpose. Today is the end of my second year in this strict regime penal camp. Perhaps I can tell you what it's like here and how I have spent these last two years. I won't bother to mention the daily state of hunger (since I have got used to it now), nor will I bother to relate to you the continual harassment and humiliation to which we are subjected (since this is not new to me either). Twice in two years I've been put into solitary confinement and three times I was denied my rights of having personal visits from my family. Many officers tell me privately and quite frankly that not only is this not their own doing, but that they cannot do anything to stop it. (For understandable reasons I won't name these men.)

This is why I've decided to write to you, Leonid Ilich. I know that this letter will not terminate my undesired pilgrimage here in prison. I know also that I can be put back into solitary confinement at any time and not only for fifteen days (our superiors already do this anyway whenever the whim takes them) but also for six months. I also know that I could be resentenced to a further term of imprisonment. I have often heard such threats from many officers. But I am ready for anything and I don't despair, but look with great serenity to the future. But your attitude disturbs me, Leonid Ilich. You have quite deliberately and consciously chosen the path of confrontation with the church.

Please permit me to relate to you some events from the past so that I can illustrate the point. On 16th May 1966 between 400 and 500 believers assembled in front of the buildings of the Central Committee of the Communist Party of the Soviet Union (CPSU). They had come together from all parts of the country to inform you about persecution and the violation of the just processes of law, about the breaking up of church services and unreasonable fines, about the confiscation of property and the removal of parental rights, in brief, to inform you that Christians in our country are citizens almost devoid of any civic rights. It seemed that there was nothing to stand in the way of having such a meeting. But events were to prove otherwise. We read in the morning newspapers of 17th May that you had flown to Vladivostok the evening before to confer the order of Lenin upon some of the inhabitants of the city. Of course we understand that your work also runs to a schedule. But you didn't even see fit to delegate to any of your co-workers the responsibility of hearing the complaints of these believers who had come so far. So instead of a dialogue with you there were arrests. Between three and four o'clock in the afternoon buses arrived at the entrance to the Central Committee building and the believers were bundled into these buses and then carted off to Lefortovo prison. Most of them were then released after fifteen days but twenty-five people were sentenced. Later on many of the members of that delegation were rearrested in the towns where they lived.

On 19th May I was arrested myself in front of the buildings of the Central Committee as I was on my way to see you. Since then more than sixteen years have passed. During this period of time I have already been sentenced three times. Each time it was because of my service for God. I'm not complaining about my lot. I thank God for the possibility of being able to contend for the truth of Christ at the defendant's bench. But there's something else that bothers me. Does this way that you've chosen, the way of confrontation with the church, serve any useful purpose either to the state as a whole or to your personal authority? I follow attentively the efforts you are making for the well-being of all people. And I wish you great success in your efforts from the bottom of my heart. But allow me to ask you a question: How can you concern yourself with the well-being of people in the rest of the world when in your own country there are many people who have been deprived of their rights, eg orphans whose fathers have been put in prison for no reason? Please allow me also to cite a few more examples of our treatment in various places.

Consider the incident which took place in 1971 in the town of Soroki. I was serving my second term of imprisonment under strict regime. It was night-time. Everyone in my section was asleep. Making the most of the quietness I knelt down between the bunks. At that time the guards were on patrol and when they saw me kneeling one of them kicked me in the side with the toecap of his boot and shouted, 'Hey, you dog, you've been sent here to learn Marxist-Leninist ideology, not to pray!' I slipped under my blanket again and they carried on their rounds, laughing.

Kishinev, in 1973. I had been home from prison for a month. Our house was searched—again. The State Prosecutor found nothing of importance in my home but did notice some entries made in my children's diaries. In them my children had written down all their secret childish thoughts. It was a carefully kept rule in our house that these diaries were strictly for the eyes of the children alone. One of the colleagues of the State Prosecutor began to read some of the entries in my son's book: 'Lord, yesterday I upset Mummy again, even though I didn't want to! Please forgive me!' Then, 'My Daddy will be coming home soon. He's a very good Daddy. When I'm big I want to be like him.' Then they began to laugh at these entries. But the little boy who was the author of these lines sat in the corner and wept uncontrollably. Even though I've written to you and tried at various times to get these diaries back it has all been to no avail . . .

Ishevsk. An elder of the ECB Church, A N Shubinin, was being tried. He was sitting in the dock. Just as every criminal has harmed someone, so this man too had five people he had 'harmed' paraded before him. All of them were children. One after the other they were summoned into the courtroom. Each one was asked, 'Do you believe that God exists?' and each one answered, 'Yes.' The answer was firm and decisive. Some deprecating remark was made before they were chased out of the courtroom. The teachers were up in arms. 'It's a disgrace that our pupils believe in God!' and they demanded that the accused be removed from society so that he couldn't hinder the building of the atheistic society.

I can cite many other similar instances. But there is no point in trying to prove to you that Christians in our country are persecuted simply because they believe in God and serve him without compromise. And why is there no point? Because it is an indisputable fact that all this is a deliberate policy directed from the top. Everywhere, be it in the courtroom, or in the press, or in personal contact with ordinary people, peaceful church services are portrayed as 'gatherings of no-gooders'. Often drunken, part-time policemen are used to break up services. And as for prison sentences, don't we all know that this too is a policy deliberately directed from the top? It seems to have been official policy to imprison one or two church officers from churches throughout the whole of the Soviet Union, from Magadan through all regions of the north.

Leonid Ilich, this letter has just one purpose: it is an attempt to normalise the relationship between the state and the church. In this letter I have expressed my personal views to you and I'm sorry that I haven't been able to express them more fully. Now no food will pass my lips until I receive an answer from you. Tomorrow I will notify the authorities of my intention. I will fast and pray until you answer this letter. If you should continue to harden your heart and show no desire to discuss these matters that I've raised (which I hope will not be the case), then I will still pray for you, even though it be the last prayer I make on earth. 'For to whom much is given much will also be expected.' And 'God will not be mocked.' So I wish you, and through you the whole of our people, the people which God has trusted to you, blessing and well-being.

This letter never received a reply, because Leonid Brezhnev died on 10 November 1982.

Chucheleny

Judge: Now let's go back more specifically to the events that took place in Chucheleny.

Khorev: I was threatened with three years' imprisonment because I had supposedly organised a procession on a certain wedding day. This is what happened. No buses were running on that day. Since we had parked our cars in the neighbouring villages, we had to walk. Scarcely had we started than the president of the local village soviet suddenly came and offered us a bus. But since there wasn't enough room in it for everyone, we let the women and children go in the bus while the rest of us set out on foot. Then we were offered four cars and so we travelled in them. So the accusation of organising a procession in the village does not apply at all to this particular situation. In any case, it's a custom in Moldavia to organise a bridal procession from the bridegroom's house to the bride's house and then back again, and no one has to get special permission for this.

Judge: Then what do you have to say about the other things that happened, as for example, the time you stayed in the church elder's house in Bendery, as well as the visits you made to Sofiyevka and Leningrad? Were you ever in these cities?

Khorev: Yes, I was in Sofiyevka in 1978. The whole way there we were followed by a Volga saloon car. Scarcely had we entered the house of our Christian friends than we were summoned to appear before the village soviet. The man who had followed us all the way from Kishinev was there. They ordered me to show my identity papers. Now what was the crime I committed? Was it, perhaps, that it took me half an hour to produce my papers? The reason I delayed was that the man in plain clothes refused to produce his own identity papers. The visits to Leningrad and Bendery were similar to the one I've just mentioned.

Judge: So you do not admit to refusing to heed a demand of the authorities?

Khorev: Of course I don't.

Judge: Do you admit that you wrote the following articles. (At this point eight articles were produced.)

Khorev: Even though I really like all of those articles, I only wrote four of them, I'm afraid. And in particular the article entitled 'Holy Disobedience' is the one for which I am being charged. In it I am accused of inciting people to disobey the legislation governing religious cults. I'd just like to say a brief word about this. Many believers have appealed to the government and to the Constitution Commission to have these laws changed. Unfortunately they have received no answer. Christians cannot submit to this legislation and for this reason it has been rejected by many churches.

Judge: You called this legislation, which expresses the viewpoint of the Party, a 'heartless and idolatrous monument'.

Khorev: I made no mention of the Party.

Judge: But the Party had a part in the formulation of this legislation.

Khorev: This particular legislation expresses the opinion of atheists. But the Party, according to the constitution of the country, concedes to both believers and to non-believers alike the same rights. Is this true or not true? If this is so, would you please publish my article 'Holy Disobedience'.

Holy Disobedience

It's torment enough to have to live in prison amongst people you don't know, but when you're also forced to desecrate the sanctity of your own heart by denying God and worshipping lifeless idols then the agony becomes even more excruciating.

This is what the Jews had to face when they were in Babylonian exile. Whether he wanted to or not, as soon as the horn sounded everyone had to prostrate himself and worship an idolatrous statue more than thirty metres high. Even though they were prisoners, the Jews still remembered the command: 'Thou shalt worship the Lord thy God and serve him alone.' How should one behave when one's liberty has been removed and daily one is forced to do that which is abhorrent to one's own soul? Whoever did not obey the command of the king risked his own life.

There were many Jews in prison and how some of them managed to escape the furnace is unknown. But we do know of three men who refused to obey the king and were reported to him. They openly disobeyed his command.

Throughout the ages it has only been the humble and courageous who have made no secret of their belonging to God and have openly confessed his name under all circumstances. These three young men were intelligent and held high posts in the court. Despite his anger the king wanted to find out for himself the reason for the offensive behaviour of his subjects.

'Are you wilfully defying my command to worship the golden idol?' asked the king. And he issued the command again.

He could hardly believe that his highly esteemed ministers would deliberately flaunt his will. He thought their behaviour must be just a fleeting aberration and so it seems he was ready to listen to their excuses and the justification for their behaviour.

'We don't have to answer you, O King.'

No wonder that Nebuchadnezzar erupted into a blind rage and had them thrown into the furnace when he heard this answer.

Experienced old men shook their greying heads saying: 'Youth! What an unnecessary risk to take! Why make yourself so vulnerable when living in a foreign country! Why on earth did they play with fire? They were promising young men and just look what they could have achieved with their lives!'

But thank God that these three young men, though they did not possess any 'experience of life', did possess a living faith in God. And because of their love for God they had no intention of deceiving the king or using ambiguous language to extricate themselves from their predicament.

These statues, these idols, were a real stumbling block for all Jews. Each one tested the faith and the hope of every Jew. Who knows how long they would have struggled with their consciences had not these three men been zealous for the God of Israel? Who knows how many more would have sinned!? And furthermore, a whole new generation of Jews born in captivity would have inherited a distorted picture of the God of Abrahám, Isaac and Jacob. The Jews themselves would only have had themselves to blame for teaching their own children idolatry and hypocrisy.

There was no skilful diplomat, scholar or magician at that time who could ever have persuaded Nebuchadnezzar that this command to worship the statue was the biggest mistake he could ever make. All arguments would have remained in vain. But God's almighty power alone, revealed through these three young faithful servants, freed the king from his blindness so that he revoked the old command to make way for a new one: the God of Shadrach, Meshach and Abednego alone was to be worshipped! It is surely a rare event in history to find a king who honestly admitted how good it was to have those in his kingdom who were 'prepared to surrender their bodies because they didn't want to worship any other god other than their own God' (Dan 3:28). Without this sacrifice on the part of these three faithful servants of God, Daniel 3:20 would never have existed: 'Praise be to the God of Shadrach, Meshach and Abednego!' From that moment on the people of God were allowed to worship their God without hindrance. From that time on the fearful no longer had to hide themselves, nor did those who clung to righteousness in their hearts have to suffer like Lot.

Praise God that Shadrach, Meshach and Abednego feared betrayal of God more than they feared the rage of the king and his furnace. Their victory causes many today to revere our God and their faithfulness encourages all who love the Lord not to worship the heartless idols of the twentieth century.

But what about us?

Not so long ago an official from the Council for Religious Affairs summoned me to his office. During our discussion he insisted that we register our church but without stating that we belonged to the Council of Churches and binding ourselves to the compulsory observance of the 1929 legislation governing religious cults.

'We are prepared to register our church,' I said. 'We have applied for registration several times. But we are not prepared to keep the 1929 legislation. I know that this will mean that we will be in a continual state of conflict with you and that we will have to spend times in imprisonment, pay huge fines and so on. But at this time we have no other alternative.'

'Christ's teaching,' I continued, 'sets as our first priority the proclamation of the message of salvation everywhere. And our right to do this is enshrined in the basic law of our land, namely in the decree about the separation of church and state.[5] But the legislation which you demand we keep is in direct contradiction to this decree and does not allow us to evangelise. It also limits our right to educate our children according to our religious convictions. The only thing it allows us to do is to hold religious services, which means that we can only pray during church services. It also means that we cannot share about Jesus Christ with anyone else. But Christ has laid the responsibility upon us not only to pastor the sheep but also to feed the lambs, that is, to feed our children. And that we will do, regardless of the consequences. According to the 1929 legislation we are not allowed to support fellow believers in any material way even though it is not only our desire but also a command of Christ to look after widows and orphans. We always have those amongst us who are suffering for the sake of following God and whose families are in need of our help.'

'But if we allowed you this right you would become too powerful,' the minister commented. 'You must keep the 1929 legislation,' he insisted, 'that is the duty of every Soviet citizen! Any violation of these laws will be dealt with in court, as you well know.'

'Yes, I know that very well. I've already been in prison twice for this. But keeping this legislation is irreconcilable with serving God as the gospel lays down, and our church will choose to serve God regardless of the persecution we receive.'

'What you should say is that it's really only you who doesn't like this legislation. The other ninety-nine per cent of Christians are quite happy with these laws and are not as rebellious as you,' he said emphatically.

'Well, should we conduct an opinion poll amongst the Christians?' I remonstrated.

'If you do you'll get another jail sentence straight away! Why are you so aggressive? Not even the churches of the AUECB complain about these laws.[6] Or if they do, no one expresses a negative opinion openly,' he remarked with a hard look which said much.

'So no one's expressing a negative opinion openly?' I thought as I left the minister. 'And that's precisely why this idol has stood in place since 1929 and has tormented the people of God, gathering around it a host of feckless worshippers.'

In order to survive and keep their prayer houses open, believers had to commit some of the greatest sins against God. At first they did not want to create any upset and thought that somehow they would be able to work around these laws. But by 1935 this silent attitude of compromise had resulted in almost all prayer houses being closed in both sections of the Protestant Church in the USSR, the evangelical and the Baptist, so that only four prayer houses in this whole vast land still remained open, namely those in Moscow, Leningrad, Novosibirsk and Ulyanovsk.

This monstrous idol has been in place for half a century and it's simply shocking to think that for half a century Christians have been bowing down to it, fully aware of their unfaithfulness to God. Only a few lone Christians have dared shed their blood and remain faithful to God. The majority of Christians have preferred to remain silent these fifty years. Others thought there was no great harm in partially keeping these laws. A third group toyed with their consciences, deciding in their hearts not to obey these laws while not saying so to anyone.

Many Christians have been plagued by their consciences because they are continually accused in press and on radio, in lectures and court rooms of violating this legislation. How many Christians have been robbed not only of their freedom but also of their lives because of their uncompromising service of God? And all this because this legislation of 1929 totally contradicts the constitution of our country, and also violates all international conventions on human rights which have been signed by our country and are legally binding on all signatories.

Before these laws were passed in our country thousands of evangelical Baptist churches were operating and the majority of them were not registered. They conducted the same services as we do today and the Christians were not regarded as criminals because of the decree that was in force. But ten years later this legislation was passed and suddenly these same Christians became criminals and were rounded up en masse in prisons. What had happened? Had the believers changed? No! When the atheists saw that they were impotent in their ideological battle against religion they decided to eradicate all faith in God by force.

'How would Shadrach, Meshach and Abednego have behaved if they had been in our place?' I thought to myself. 'Would they have prevailed upon us that we be silent and behave "reasonably"?' Never! They didn't remain silent before Nebuchadnezzar otherwise he would have interpreted their silence as assent to worshipping his idolatrous statue. Nor could you imagine that these Old Testament men would have answered the king ambiguously: 'Well, thank you, O King, for your warning. We will bear that in mind in the future.' We know full well that for everyone who compromises to save his own skin there is one who sacrifices everything to follow the Lord faithfully and to show love to his people. Whatever physical punishment we might have to bear, sincere Christians must always say: 'No never! Never will I bow down to any idol! Never and in no way will I ever tolerate a rival to my Lord! He alone it is whom I will serve; he alone it is whom I will worship!'

This article was first published in Vestnik Istiny issue no. 1, 1978.

Judge: So you're opposed to this legislation. What precisely do you disagree with?

Khorev: Firstly, I disagree with any representative of the Council of Religious Affairs, an atheist, being given the authority by this legislation to remove a person who has been previously elected by the church for a particular ministry. Just to quote one example, when our church was applying for registration, G F Eksar was elected to become a member of the executive committee of the church. But the local representative for Religious Affairs removed him, giving the reason that his voice was too deep!

Secondly, this legislation makes us responsible for keeping the relevant authorities informed about our inner-church matters. This is impossible for us because such information would only be used to destroy the church. And when we want to hold a special meeting in the church we first of all have to get the permission of these authorities. However, this permission is only given if we submit a written agenda ahead of time. This legislation also forbids the formation of an orchestra, a youth choir and the holding of ladies' meetings. The whole legislation was framed during the era of the Stalinist cult of personality, and even though Stalin has long been condemned, these oppressive laws still remain in force fifty years later.

Judge: So you disagree with these laws and you are going to deliberately flaunt them?

Khorev: Yes, but not with malicious intent, just simply because of our own convictions.

Public Prosecutor (turning to Khorev): Haven't you finished yet?

Khorev: Please, I've waited for months for this meeting.

Public Prosecutor: These laws forbid the holding of services in non-registered houses. They only permit the holding of funeral services in the houses of deceased persons if you've first of all obtained permission from the authorities. Is this why you flaunt the law and also refuse registration, to escape the control of the state? Does this now mean that you are publicly making known your refusal, in future, to keep these laws?

Khorev: Yes, it does, and that for as long as these laws give atheists the right to interfere in the internal affairs of the church.

Public Prosecutor: Then are we to regard this attitude of yours as a call to Christians to disobey that law?

Khorev: Well, if that's the way you want to see it.

The Importance of Material and Spiritual Support

A letter to friends abroad.

Dear Friends,

We know full well how much concern you have shown in your countries for the needs of the Christians in the Soviet Union. I single out the Soviet Union because our own horizons are so narrow that we get embarrassed when we talk about other countries. We know so very little, perhaps the odd incident here and there, about the difficult conditions prevailing, say, in China, or in other countries ravaged by hunger and deprivation. So when your help reaches us, dear brothers and sisters, we automatically turn to the Lord and ask, 'Lord are we really the ones who most need this help? Aren't there other people in the world who have even less to eat than we do and who need the Word of God even more than we do!? O Lord, why are we the recipients of such grace?'

And it's not so much the gifts that bring us the greatest joy, but much more the thought of the givers, of those people who have sent them to us with such love.

We are especially overjoyed, dear ones, when we receive your gifts of the thousands of Bibles in our various languages. We know that you have to pay for each book. We know that there are friends taking great risks to transport this literature across the borders. It's a matter of real concern to us to hear of the arrest in Kiev of three Christian friends (we don't even know their names). We know that they were arrested as they were bringing the Holy Scriptures to us. Thankfully they were allowed to go free but the whole stock of literature was confiscated. Some have even had their cars taken away.

This is all part of enduring material and moral harm. I should not really speak of 'moral harm' for it is a great joy and privilege to be arrested and deported from a country for distributing the Word of God, especially when in that country the Word of God is maligned, confiscated and hated by some, but so fervently loved by others that they are prepared to die for it.

I would like to point you back to the distant years of the thirties.

At that time we were living in Leningrad. There were four of us children. Our parents were in a very difficult situation due to the fact that the authorities had confiscated their personal identity cards because they were believers. So they had to leave Leningrad. Also if a person loses his personal identity card he cannot get a job.

We did not starve that year in the sense of there being nothing to buy in the shops. But rather we just had no means of supporting ourselves since no one could get a job. Other Christians found themselves in a very pressurised situation as well. Many of them were arrested, while others fled and still others went into hiding. Some were forcibly deported from Leningrad. One incident in particular was clearly stamped on my mind since I was a child and my memory was still very impressionable. I can't remember the exact year, month or day on which this event happened. Nor do I remember how old I was at the time. Perhaps I was five. But I remember on the particular day in question my mother saying to my father, 'There is no one else I can borrow money from because I owe money to everyone. I just can't bear the thought of going out and asking again. Can-you get us through this day?'

My father was a man with a cheerful disposition who loved life and as far as I can remember he had always trusted the Lord and cast all the worries of everyday life upon him. So he said, 'Grunya (which is a pet name for Agrippina, my mother's name), don't worry, I'll take on the responsibility of getting us through this day.'

So mother went into the kitchen to wash or do something else. But one thing was clear: she definitely never went there to prepare food even though it was midday, because there was no food to make ready. Father read something to us, told us a story. Finally we sang some psalms together.

Mother came in and said, 'I thought that you'd gone out to find some food for the children to eat. How long can we let the children go hungry like this?'

Father replied, 'Don't worry, dearest, we've committed the matter to the Lord and now we're looking to him to supply, even directly from heaven. We've told Jesus that we don't want to be in debt because we can't repay the debts. Nor do we want to go out begging because we have a wonderful Lord. So we've stretched out our hand to him today and have asked him to supply. We've just finished reading the Scriptures where it says that he will not give a stone to the one who asks for bread and he will not give a serpent to the one who asks him for fish. So go and do your work, dearest, while we wait with joyful expectation.' I remember that mother muttered something to herself because she couldn't quite get the hang of this whole thing. There was only one thing she saw: the children were hungry and needed to eat. So she went out.

At about four o'clock someone rang the bell. Father went to answer it. The postman had come. 'A parcel's just arrived,' father said. The parcel had come from the USA. Naturally we had no correspondence with anyone from abroad since at this time of the century people had very few foreign contacts. Well, who had sent us this parcel then? I don't know to this day. But the parcel had come. I can still remember what it looked like and what was in it. There was a pair of shoes for mother which fitted her exactly (her own had just been completely worn out). Then there was food and five golden roubles which could be used to buy things in the special barter-and-exchange shops. Father gave mother all the money and said, 'Dearest one, go to the nearest shop and spend the whole five roubles. Buy the best things that you can find and don't hold back. Today we cast ourselves directly on heaven's resources and the Lord has supplied our need. So today let's celebrate. It doesn't matter if people say that we don't know how to handle money, or that we throw money about and don't know how to make it last. No, no it doesn't matter. Today is a day of celebration and the Lord himself is inviting us to it.' We knelt down again and prayed. I remember those prayers very well. When mother came back she put everything on the table. There were our favourite cakes, cream rolls, and then there were other delicious items which today are commonplace to us but at that time they were very special treats.

When it was evening, father said, 'Children, we have eaten our fill but there's still a lot left on the table. Should we keep this all for ourselves for the days to come? I suggest that tomorrow we invite other families who are in the same predicament as we are and are starving. Perhaps they have been asking the Lord to supply their needs.' We eagerly agreed with him even though mother muttered under her breath, 'If we give everything away what will we do later on?' Father answered her, 'Grunya, this is our banquet. It's a banquet which the Lord has prepared for us. So let's invite all the other families who are in need to come and share.' Finally he told us the story of the manna which fell from heaven for the people of Israel and how everyone collected as much as he needed for that day. That was the first time I really took note of that story.

At lunchtime the next day our room was full of children of our own age, all as wretched as us. Their parents had also had their personal ID cards removed and so had been driven out of Leningrad. Some had lost their fathers. Father pointed to the richly laden table and asked, 'What do you think? Who do you think put all this on our table?' Everyone shrugged their shoulders. 'No rich man would have thought of this and blessed our home in such a way. No, it was the Lord himself who did this.' And then he told them what had happened the previous day. Everyone was really impressed. We prayed and sat down to eat again.

Dear friends, there's just one last thing I'd like to say to you. God will reward you according to the riches of his grace for the generosity you have shown to the Christian church in the Soviet Union. May the Lord grant to you a rich harvest from what you have sown in the past. To him be the honour for all eternity.

Further Cross-examination

Public Prosecutor: Have you been informed as to the verdict of our examination of your articles?

Khorev: Yes.

Public Prosecutor: Are you agreed with this verdict?

Khorev: I am in principle against the idea of my articles being appraised by the Society for the Spread of Scientific Knowledge because this society is a totally atheistic one.

Public Prosecutor: So you're not agreed. Some while ago in Leningrad it was demanded that children be taught the 'laws of God' in school. Is this your desire too?

Khorev: Our Council of Churches has written a letter to the government about this matter. I think that any form of compulsion is a bad thing. We are not for the compulsory teaching of God's laws neither are we for the compulsory attendance of our children at atheistic lessons. I simply wish that the 'laws of God' and 'atheism' were both subjects that were taught in our schools and that each child was free to choose the one he or she wanted to attend.

Public Prosecutor: Mikhail Ivanovich, do you hold children's meetings and young people's meetings?

Khorev: I don't wish to answer that question.

The judge ordered a recess and then for the next witnesses to be called. The first witness to be summoned was Isaak, a student in the sixth year of the Medical High School in Kishinev. He admitted to knowing Mikhail Khorev.

The judge drew his attention to the clause in the law making the refusal to give evidence or the giving of false evidence a punishable offence.

Judge: Will you please relate to us the events of August 1976.

Isaak: It was a Sunday. I was going to a lake with my friend. As we approached the tent I recognised the man who invited us to come in. I quickly ascertained that we were in a Christian meeting. They were waiting for Mikhail Ivanovich. Children and young people were present. People were singing and playing instruments and then some poetry was read aloud. At that moment the police came. They ordered the meeting to stop.

Mikhail Ivanovich, who had in the meantime arrived, addressed all those present: 'They are trying to stop our service. What do you think we should do? Carry on?' Everyone nodded assent. One person was acting in a particularly suspicious way and photographing all the police officials and their accomplices who were there.

A member of the judicial committee: So they quite deliberately photographed this incident?

Isaak: Yes.

Judge: Were children present?

Isaak: I only saw two. The man who was taking the photographs had his two children with him.

Judge: Who was leading the meeting?

Isaak: Mikhail Ivanovich.

Judge: What did he say?

Isaak: He preached and said that they were to tell people about God and to win them for their sect.

Judge: Were you able to ascertain the reason why the service was forbidden?

Isaak: They were told that they were a sect which had splintered off from the official Baptist Union.

Attorney: Did you sign a protocol?

Isaak: Yes.

Judge to Khorev: Would you like to add anything to this?

Khorev: I am not contesting that I led the service. As for the photographs, it was not only us who were taking photographs but the authorities too were photographing everything. Isn't that so, Isaak? (Isaak confirmed this fact.)

Khorev: In my messages I was not calling for people to proselytise for our sect but rather to witness about Christ.

Judge to Isaak: Here's the protocol but no mention is made of you.

Isaak: Perhaps it was because I was in the crowd.

Judge to Khorev: When did the separation, or split, between yourselves and the All-Union Council of the Evangelical Christian Baptists take place?

Khorev: I find it objectionable to speak in this court about the relationships between Christians.

The next witness to be called was B S Loginov who was the secretary of the village soviet in Chucheleny.

Judge: Do you know the accused?

Loginov: Yes, I have seen him before.

Judge: When did you see him?

Loginov: At the wedding held in Kiriyak's house in Chucheleny. We came to the house to tell them that we were prepared to lay on transport for them, but they set off by foot.

(This was the sort of unclear and meaningless evidence that was used to convict the accused.)

Public Prosecutor: Did the people have radios with them?

Loginov: Yes and they had them on very loud.

Public Prosecutor: Did they receive a warning?

Loginov: Not from me but they did from the president of the village soviet.

Public Prosecutor: Were there many people there?

Loginov: Approximately 200. They were together from morning until evening, singing and praying.

Public Prosecutor: What did the children do?

Loginov: They sang and they played.

Public Prosecutor: What were the loud speakers used for?

Loginov: I don't know.

Public Prosecutor: Why did you specifically go to Mikhail Ivanovich and to the bridal company?

Loginov: Because they were the ones leading the procession. When we told them that we had arranged transport for them, Khorev turned round and asked the others, 'Shall we believe them?' All replied, 'No.' And so they walked on.

Judge: Are there many Christians in your village?

Loginov: Approximately forty, all of them registered I think.

Judge: You said that you could really hear what was going on. What could you hear?

Loginov: The music—in fact, everything. It was all religious stuff.

Judge: And what did Khorev say?

Loginov: He said that they had all been able to gather together for the wedding despite the opposition of the Devil.

Judge: So the whole village heard him say that?

Loginov: Yes.

Judge: To whom was Khorev referring when he used the word 'Devil'? Did he mean the village authorities?

Loginov: Probably. I assume that's what he meant.

Judge to Khorev: To whom were you referring when you used the word 'Devil'?

Khorev: There is one God and there is one Devil. There are good people and there are evil people.

Judge: Who, according to your opinion, are these 'evil people'?

Khorev: Well, for example, if the State Prosecutor wishes me good, then he's a good man. But if he wishes me evil, then he is an evil man. The same goes for me and for you, your Honour.

Defence lawyer to Loginov: Do you know whether the marriage ceremony was registered at the local registry office?

Loginov: I don't know, I don't think so.

Khorev to Loginov: Will you tell the court whether the loud speakers were in the tent or outside of the tent?

Loginov: In the tent.

Khorev: And could everything be heard in the whole village?

Loginov: Well . . . no, but it could be heard in the immediate vicinity.

Khorev: Would you like to tell us the village bus timetable.

Loginov: Buses travel at 11.00, 14.30 and 18.00 hours.

Khorev: Could you confirm to us whether or not the buses were running according to schedule that day?

Loginov: Well, I don't know.

The other witnesses testified in similar fashion. The testimonies were all extremely one-sided since they all belonged to various organs of state or to the police authorities. One woman, a former collaborator with the police, even testified that the Christians had hurled offensive and abusive language at the authorities. Such testimonials only confirmed that the witnesses knew that they could spread any lies or calumnies they wished about Christians with total impunity.

The second day of the proceedings continued with the hearing of witnesses. Some of the witnesses' statements contradicted one another. Then Mikhail Khorev was questioned.

Judge: Do you admit that you described the legislation governing religious cults as a 'heartless and idolatrous monument' in your articles?

Khorev: Yes, of course I do.

Judge: Why did you separate from the All-Union Council of the Evangelical Christian Baptists in 1961?

Khorev: That is an inner-church matter and the State Prosecutor has no right to deal with this question.

Judge: Why did you tell the Christians your life-story?

Khorev: At that time I was speaking about my mother. And I was recounting how a mother, herself undernourished and exhausted, gave us her last piece of bread during the Leningrad blockade.

Judge: But non-Christian mothers did the same.

Khorev: I was speaking in general about mother-love, without grouping mothers into Christian and non-Christian mothers.

Prepare the Way of the Lord

Although the gain received from study of the Word of God is unquestionably very great and knowledge of Scripture is imperative, one doesn't need to have had a theological education or have been a Bible student long in order to prepare the hearts of unbelievers for receiving the Lord Jesus Christ. But if a person has not experienced the power of God in his life or does not know his strength and if he has not been born from above, then any testimony about Christ is out of the question.

Before we could receive the Word, the Lord Jesus Christ had to send someone ahead to prepare the way, someone who was concerned for our salvation. Do you remember who that person was for you? Do you know him? In my case it was my mother, by her words and deeds.

It was December 1941 in Leningrad. Our father was no longer with us since he had died in prison for the sake of the Word of God. It was the very difficult time of the blockade. We had been condemned to death by starvation. There were four families living in our communal dwelling. We had neither electricity nor water.

My mother worked in a hospital. When she came home in the morning she would come to our bedside to see whether we were still alive. Our room was unheated and so we all slept in one bed. After she had assured herself that God's grace had kept us through the night she would kneel down by the bedside. We would get out of bed with some difficulty and kneel down next to her. There was a certain order in our praying, starting with mother and then with the older children. I can no longer remember what mother prayed but I do remember that she would always say, 'Lord, I thank you that you love us.' After praying I would crawl back under the blankets and think, 'Why did mother say that the Lord loves us so much? If only she had brought us a piece of bread home today—at least that! But she has come home with empty hands.'

And so day followed day. I still remember when mother brought us home a small piece of cheese. She divided it into four small portions and then left the room. I did not understand why she only cut it into quarters. She had left herself out.

Her motherly instructions always remained in my consciousness even in later life. She spoke to me so often and so convincingly about Christ that I could never remain indifferent towards him. Thanks to her motherly care, Bible reading became a much loved pastime with me.

One evening before my conversion I came home late from work.

'Young man,' she said to me. 'I'm peeling potatoes and I want you to read aloud from the Bible for me.'

'Well, why don't you read it yourself?' I said evasively.

'Well, first of all, I'd have to look for my glasses and you want to eat, don't you? So why don't you read while I prepare supper?'

'Well, let me peel the potatoes and you read,' I resisted.

'Young man, I want to hear you read. Do you really find it very exciting reading when I have to spell the words?'

'All right,' I conceded. 'What part shall I read from?'

'First of all, read from the Sermon on the Mount . . . '

I knew what that meant. The Sermon on the Mount was three whole chapters! And for mother that was just the beginning. I scrambled my meagre resources of patience together and began to read aloud. First of all I read without my heart being in it, really in an inhibited fashion and without joy. I got through to the fifth chapter and then the sixth and the seventh . . . by then there was no holding me back. I read the eighth chapter, then the ninth because I just had to find out what happened next.

Mother had not only peeled the potatoes but had finished the whole supper. Then she invited me to join her at the table. But I could not tear myself away and raced along the lines. I did not know myself what had happened to me that evening. But from that time on the Old and New Testaments became my favourite books. It had been my mother who had helped me discover the fascination of the Word of God.

Once on the quayside at Khabarovsk (I was on my way to visit some Christian families) I fell into conversation with a young man while waiting for the steamer to come. He was travelling to the gold mines in the far north.

'How far you've travelled!' I said in amazement.

'Well, it's because circumstances have dictated it,' the young man sighed.

'You're still so young! Did you really have to leave your relatives and acquaintances to seek your fortune at the other end of the world?'

'If you knew my mother, then you'd understand why anyone would run away from her!' the lad answered, obviously trying to awaken my sympathy.

'Does she drink a lot then or did she not look after you properly?'

'No, but she's just so extremely pious. It's just imposs-ible to live around her. She is continually jabbing my conscience and lamenting that I don't believe in God and weeping that I am lost without God. Whenever I entered the house she would begin to sing religious songs and to read the Bible aloud.'

'And is this the only reason you decided to leave your parents' home?'

'Yes, I finally summoned the courage to tell her that I would never become a Christian. "You go your way, mother, and I'll go mine," I said, briefly and to the point. She began to weep and went into her room. I couldn't sleep the whole night long. I saw that her light was on in her room and that she wasn't sleeping either. After a while I decided to go and see what she was doing there in the middle of the night. She was on her knees praying. Well, that wasn't anything unusual! "So just let her pray," I thought to myself. At four o'clock in the morning I had another look and she was still on her knees praying. If she was spending such a long time praying for me I thought I must really have blown it with her, and so I couldn't stay a moment longer in the house. I wrote her a note saying I was leaving home to earn money and at six o'clock in the morning I had already left the house.'

'Well, where are you running away to? You went away to escape her words and her songs but you can never escape from a praying mother. Prayer is a power that is so all-pervasive that there's no way you can hide from it, either at the other end of the world or even under the earth! Prayer will reach you wherever you choose to go!'

'Are you a Christian too, then?' he asked with mixed amazement and annoyance.

'Yes.'

'Well, that's just fine. I'm trapped again!' he said with rising anger and clenching his fists.

'What do you mean "trapped again"?'

'Well I've only been on the road for two weeks and you're already the third Christian I've met!' the young man retorted angrily and went on his way.

He should have boarded the same boat as I but as soon as we were allowed on board he walked up and down the quayside nervously. I knew that he had no intention of continuing his journey. Perhaps it was because I was an unwelcome travelling companion for him or perhaps it was because he had decided not to travel to the far north but rather to return home. But however he decided, the prayers of his mother were having an effect on the heart of her wayward son and if the mother held firm to her faith then her prayers would surely be answered. She was a true 'preparer of the way' for her son.

This article was first published in Vestnik Istiny issue no. 1 1984

Mrs Mevshe's Testimony

Mrs V Mevshe, a Christian and a worker in the village Sofiyevka, was the next to appear in the witness box.

Judge: Do you know the accused?

Mevshe: Yes, I know him. He is a very good brother.

Judge: Did you know him previously?

Mevshe: Yes.

Judge: Would you like to tell us what happened in the Arnanta's flat?

Mevshe: Well, that's a while ago. We had a meeting in his house.

Judge: What sort of meeting was it that you had?

Mevshe: It was a meeting of Christian friends.

Judge: How did these Christian friends regard the accused?

Mevshe: They regarded him as a brother.

Judge: In your village are there registered and unregistered Christians?

Mevshe: I don't know.

Judge: How long were you at school?

Mevshe: How long? Well, long enough to read!

Judge: Do you know it's forbidden for unregistered Christians to meet together?

Mevshe: I know that the church is separate from the state.

Judge: Have you ever read the periodical entitled *Vestnik Istiny* ('The Messenger of Truth') and have you ever heard of Khorev's articles?

Mevshe: No.

Khorev explained that it could well be possible that the witness knew nothing of the periodical *Vestnik Istiny*. This periodical was produced illegally and only 15,000 copies were published. Khorev testified that this amount was by no means sufficient for all the Christians to have one each. It could be that copies did not reach the village where the witness lived. In the future however, testified Khorev, they would seek to publish more so that Sofiyevka too would be able to get copies of the periodical.

Judge: Did Khorev read aloud at that meeting?

Mevshe: Yes, he read from the Bible.

Associate Judge: Do you have any sort of calendar of your services?

Mevshe: We meet together every Sunday.

Judge: You are obliged to tell us who leads these meetings.

Mevshe: Well, I'm afraid I won't tell you. That's a secret of the fellowship.

Judge: A secret of which fellowship?

Mevshe: Of our fellowship.

Judge: Do you know that you can be penalised for refusing to give evidence?

Mevshe: I will tell you anything, as long as it is necessary evidence.

Judge: Do you know why Khorev is being tried? I'll read you something from his article called 'Holy Disobedience'. Khorev writes in it that the legislation governing religious cults (which he calls a 'heartless and idolatrous monument') gathers around it a host of feckless and spiritually dead people. Do you believe that too?

Mevshe: No, I don't think so. But I do think brother Khorev is a good brother.

Judge: When did you become a Christian?

Mevshe: In 1968.

Public Prosecutor: Why weren't you a Christian before this?

Mevshe: I simply didn't understand what the faith was all about. Then I began to read the Bible and I began to believe.

Public Prosecutor: Who enticed you to become a Christian?

Mevshe: God.

Public Prosecutor, pointing to the accused: Not this 'brother'?

Mevshe: I didn't know him at that time.

Public Prosecutor: Do you know why the service was forbidden at that time?

Mevshe: No, I don't know.

Public Prosecutor: Do you understand that the state must find out your secrets, otherwise you could be conducting espionage under the guise of religion?

Mevshe: What! Us conducting espionage? (An outbreak of laughter in the courtroom.)

Public Prosecutor: Do you have any idea what agency might be controlling and manipulating you all?

Mevshe: No, I have no idea, but obviously you have.

Public Prosecutor: You speak about God. God lives in heaven. But there are many sects and I see that you don't really know yourself what you believe.

Gypsies Know How to Pray

Life in one gypsy church of the ECB federation.

As a result of a revival amongst the gypsies of Trans-Carpathia a young church came into being and in 1978–79 a further seven gypsies were added to this church. But it was a special matter for joy that for the first time a gypsy woman came to faith. It is much harder for such women to come to know the Lord because they are so bound by palmistry, deceitfulness and an over-concern for their families.

On 27th July 1979 these gypsies were baptised together with some other recent converts in a neighbouring Ukrainian assembly. Approximately 500 believers came to the riverside. There were also over 300 uniformed policemen, not to mention auxiliary police. As the gypsies descended into the water to seal their holy covenant with their Saviour the army of atheists got really upset. 'Now look what they're up to! They're baptising gypsies!'

The Christians in these gypsy churches are very courageous. The church services which are very well attended surge with deep passion and emotion. The young preachers, only converted three years previously, proclaim the Word of God with simplicity and persuasiveness. No matter how big the rooms in which the services take place, they are always jam-packed. After four or five people have prayed aloud, the whole assembly prays the Lord's Prayer. Finally, at the end of the service, they sing a communal hymn: 'The grace of our Lord Jesus Christ . . . ' They love singing Christian songs, both in their own language as well as in Russian. The song 'Lord teach me to pray . . . ' which is sung in our assemblies, is now being sung in gypsy churches too and after they have sung all the verses in their own gypsy language they sing them all over again in Russian. Hardly anyone needs to use a song book because they know the songs off by heart, since most of them cannot read or write.

As soon as a visiting preacher arrives at a gypsy camp all the adults and children come running out of their houses. They leave their work and gather to hear the Word of God late into the night, for as long as the preacher is able to speak. It seems that gypsies never get tired.

During one such visit the service began at eight o'clock in the morning. It was only late into the evening that the first women began to depart, after the preacher had hinted that it was high time that the service closed. But left to themselves, they would not have gone.

I also used to visit gypsy families. Once I was visiting a brother at eleven o'clock at night. His wife was a recent convert and they had five children. About thirty other people accompanied me to their house. It had two large rooms, one where the man did his work and the other a living-room. I read a few verses from the Holy Scriptures and then called them to prayer. During the prayer time a shrill whistling emitted from the corner of the room. Everyone looked around and an old man was lying there on a camp bed. He looked in a terrible state. His face was pock-marked with blue blotches, evidence that he was a habitual drinker. He was dressed in rags and his hair was matted and unkempt.

'Who's that?' I asked the man of the house. 'Is he a relative of yours?'

'No. I don't know him at all.'

'What do you mean you don't know him? He's here in your house, in your living-room and you say you don't know him?'

'There's an extremely sharp frost outside. He would have frozen to death if he had stayed outside so I invited him in to stay the night.'

'How can you stand such a man who whistles so loudly?'

'What else could I do? When it's as cold outside as it is today you'd even let a dog come into the warm. So how could we refuse this man?'

After we exchanged a few more words we both knelt down to pray.

'Damn you!' screamed the old man as loud as he could.

This picture stuck a long while in my memory. My wife, I thought, would never have allowed such a person, who cursed and whistled during the prayer time, to stay overnight. But then I checked myself. What has this got to do with my wife? I myself would never have allowed such a person into my house either. I realised how large-hearted these simple people were!

Gypsy Christians love to testify to others about their faith in Jesus and they make use of every opportunity. Once, a brother went into a canteen. He wanted to tell people about the Lord but did not know how to begin. He placed his meal down on the table and prayed aloud. He thanked God for the abundant harvest, for his health and that they had never experienced famine. He simply thanked the Lord for everything that came into his head and heart. In the meantime a deathly hush descended on the room as everyone listened intently to the gypsy's prayers. He thought that he would be bombarded with questions after his prayer but people just cast embarrassed looks in his direction and continued to eat in silence. The brother started his meal and decided to thank the Lord aloud for his food. The eyes of all were riveted on him. 'What are you all looking at me for?' he said turning to them all after he had prayed. 'Is it strange to you that a gypsy should pray? It is to me. How can it be that I, a gypsy, can speak with God but you have never learned how to pray? Haven't you seen chickens lifting their heads up to heaven after they've foraged around and swallowed their food? You're all eating away and not one of you has prayed to God to say thank you. The ox knows his master's crib but human beings do not know their God who gives them so much to eat every day, who gives them their health and maintains their life.'

Their prayers are simply wonderful and so penetrating that even experienced preachers of the Word can learn from them.

Before the gypsies repented, their wives used to go through the villages and steal chickens. But when the men came to know the Lord they decided to follow the example of Zacchaeus and repay each one for the loss incurred. One autumn one of the gypsies made a big box and put all his chickens in it. He put the box on his horse and cart and drove it through the village. He knocked on the first farmer's door. 'Excuse me, ma'am! Could you come here a moment?' People came running from the neighbouring houses thinking that the gypsy wanted to sell something. Then he asked, 'Listen, have any gypsies stolen any chickens from you? Have you lost any chickens?'

'Well, yes, we have lost some,' the farmer's wife answered and did not quite know what to make of these remarks.

'Well, I don't know how many chickens my wife stole off you. Here, I'll give you three back. I won't steal any more and I won't allow her to steal either. I've become a believer in God and have stopped stealing. Don't look so nonplussed, just take them. God has forgiven me and I would like you to forgive me too.'

The lady was quite taken aback. There was a real din going on with the chickens squawking, and people coming from all the neighbouring farms, so the gypsy Christian stood on his cart and began to preach about Christ. Some received the chickens, others refused them, but he went on through the village knocking on other farm doors until he had given away the last chicken. And he shared with everyone that it was God who had made him into a good and honest man.

Some time later another gypsy was driving his horse and cart through a village when he heard the sound of singing and music and a whole lot of noise. A family celebration was taking place and he felt a desperate urge to tell these people about his Saviour Jesus. As soon as he came into the courtyard the whole drunken company gathered around him.

'Hey, gypo, dance for us!' And everyone began to clap.

'I can't dance.'

'What sort of gypsy are you if you can't dance. Well, read our palms then!'

'I can't do that either.'

'Well, tell us what you can do!'

'I can pray to God.'

'Well, that's interesting. Let's see you pray then. We know you're having us on and kidding us along.'

'Right then, I'll pray for you all here on the spot.'

'Okay, pray, come on, pray! We've never heard a gypsy pray before.'

'Well, first of all, let me ask you all to kneel down together with me.'

'Come on then, let's kneel down. It'll be a real hoot,' they laughed.

Whether it was just a joke or whether they had other reasons for doing it, everyone knelt down.

'But I did not think it was funny,' the gypsy told us later. 'So I closed my eyes and began to ask the Lord to have grace upon these people. I prayed deeply that God might forgive them their sins. When I stood up several of them had tears in their eyes but I was really sorry that no one prayed the prayer of commitment after me.'

The gypsies told me of an incident that happened during one of their non-Christian weddings. Everyone was in very high spirits and people were dancing. According to gypsy custom no one may disturb this festive spirit. However, one Christian brother just could not look on and see his friends grieving the Lord's heart, so he decided to tell them about eternal life and eternal joy in heaven. He filled his pockets with stones and stepped into the midst of the dancers!

'I'd like to tell you about the Lord! Please listen!' he shouted above the noise and din. 'God's got such joy in store for you! He will forgive you your sins and take you to heaven! Do you want this joy?' he asked, turning to the bride and groom. There was some confusion and suddenly the main gypsy leader came over to him. This man was the chief of the clan and everyone had to obey him.

'Why have you come to disturb the celebrations?'

'I want to tell you about the Lord.'

'Listen, drink a glass of wine and enjoy yourself. But if you want to do any more than this, come tomorrow, but don't disturb us now.'

'But tomorrow might be too late. We could die tomorrow. I want to tell you today.'

The gypsy chief grabbed the Christian by the lapels but the Christian brother quite simply said, 'Chief, stretch your hands out to me.' The chief dutifully stretched out his hands and the Christian brother cupped them together and asked, 'Do you use bad language?'

'Yes, I do,' he replied. So the brother took a stone from his pocket and placed it into the chief's hands.

'Do you smoke?'

'Yes, I do!' The brother put another stone into his hands.

'Is your wife a fortune-teller?'

'Yes, she is.' He placed a third stone into his hands.

'Do you steal?'

'Yes, I do.' A fourth stone was put into his hands.

'Do you fight? Do you drink vodka?' Gradually the stones were emptied from the right and from the left pocket and were placed into the hands of the gypsy chief.

'When you appear before the judgement seat of God, then these stones will testify against you that you are a sinner and you didn't allow me to tell others about the Lord. You must repent, Chief, or you will die in your sins. You must pray that God will forgive you. God loves you.'

He just simply said these few words and then left. The old chief stood there for a long time in the midst of the company looking at the stones in his hands, and then to the gypsy who was disappearing in the distance.

The methods the gypsies use to preach the gospel are inimitable. Sometimes they preach in our churches too. In 1979 in the church at Peressyp, near Odessa, a service was in progress. Many police officials were present. It was a rather noisy meeting and when the gypsy preacher got up into the pulpit one of the officers began to speak angrily against him.

'Please be quiet, officer!' said the preacher. 'I've got to speak to you about God and you must listen to me.' At that moment an almighty hullabaloo broke out so that the preacher had to pause awhile until some measure of order had been restored. Then he continued, 'Brothers and sisters . . . I've forgotten what I was going to say now, so let's pray that God will give me the word he wants me to speak.' After praying, this brother went on to preach.

Once, when I was in one of their camps, I heard a gypsy preaching. 'Is there anyone who wants to repent?' the young preacher asked his congregation. 'Who wants to live in the heavenly Jerusalem? God has a Book of Life and there are still empty pages left in this book for God to write your name in it. Who would like his name to be written into this book?'

A fifteen-year-old lad stood up and said, 'I would!'

'Do you know that you are a sinner?' the preacher asked him.

'Yes.'

'Do you know that the blood of Jesus washes away your sins?'

'Yes.'

'Then please kneel down.'

They just go straight to the point and don't beat about the bush. We all took part in that prayer. It was in the gypsy language which we did not understand but in our spirits we knew that the same God who understands us and saves us can also save these dear people. They are as precious to God as the rest of us.

Perhaps gypsies are despised because they lie and steal but when they turn to God in repentance they receive new birth. Then they turn away completely from their old way of life and witness gladly to the Lord amongst their fellows. Thanks be to God for his inexpressible gift!

The Final Hours

Judge (turning to Khorev): Who financed your journeys?

Khorev: On that matter, I am accountable only to those who commissioned me to do this work.

Judge: Would you please name the members of the Council of Churches and also give their addresses?

Khorev: You can obtain these from the circular letter which is distributed amongst the brothers.

Judge: Do you really only produce 15,000 copies of the periodical *Vestnik Istiny*?

Khorev: You know that we have to produce this periodical under very difficult circumstances. It could be that we print a few more or a few less than 15,000. They're often confiscated. But I'm really glad to say that a complete edition of the issue containing the article 'Holy Disobedience' was distributed amongst the Christians.

Further witnesses were called who were either atheists or state sympathisers. Christians were accused of holding meetings in the woods during the May holidays which disturbed the peace of other 'normal' citizens. The judges were particularly concerned to establish the fact that the public order had been disturbed and that Khorev had stirred up young men to refuse military service. Mikhail Khorev was then forced to ask additional questions of these witnesses.

Khorev to one of the witnesses: Did I really call upon people to refuse military service?

Witness: No, what you said was that when those who were presently doing military service returned home, they should join you.

Khorev: Did I say that you had to refuse to bear arms?

Witness: No.

Khorev: When were these young people taught about military service? While they were kneeling?

Witness: No, after that.

Towards the end of the second day of the hearing, Khorev's defence lawyer who had compulsorily been assigned him, made a remarkable and impressive defence on Khorev's behalf.

'Your Honour, this is a unique trial. The accused, Mikhail Ivanovich Khorev, is charged with violating four articles of the law of the MSSR. These four articles are the following:

'Article 142/II: "A person, once found guilty of violating the laws governing the separation of church and state, convicted again for the same offence, will be liable to imprisonment for up to three years."

'Article 143/I: "Any activity, or the leading of any activity, having the semblance of religious ceremony or religious proclamation, that in any way causes damage to other citizens' health or in any other way injuriously affects them will carry a maximum sentence of five years (plus also possible confiscation of property). This same penalty applies to any activity which encourages citizens to refrain from exercising their civic duties for the common good."

'Article 203/I: "A systematic dissemination of deliberately falsified information, in either verbal or written form, slandering the Soviet political or social systems, shall carry a maximum sentence of three years' imprisonment."

'Article 203/III: "The organisation of or active participation in any group activities which seriously violate public order or can be construed as blatantly disregarding the legal demands of the instituted authorities shall carry a maximum sentence of three years' imprisonment."

'Khorev is accused of having instructed children in religious matters. In reaching this verdict the court assumes that children were present at the meetings. But the relevant paragraph of the law states that only systematic, and I stress systematic, teaching of children in matters of religion is a punishable offence. The presence

66

of children in services is, on the contrary, not an offence that is punishable by law, nor does the law forbid it. Failure to register organised religious meetings with the authorities is technically an administrative offence. The accused was charged with such an offence but has already paid his fifty rouble fine. However, the same violation cannot be punished twice. This is why it is legally impossible for the accused to be charged again for this offence. I plead with you to acquit Khorev because the charges against him are not substantiated. The court should bear in mind that all the offences with which the accused has been charged happened between two and a half and four years ago and are no longer punishable by law.

'Moreover, Khorev is accused of having written eight articles which appeared in the illegal periodical *Vestnik Istiny*.[7] But this periodical is published by a group which has splintered off from the mainstream of the Baptists. He is also being accused of inciting people in messages which were supposedly taped to disobey the legislation governing religious cults, as well as to desist from exercising their civil and social responsibilities. These tapes have not been played during this court hearing and are not in evidence. Furthermore, Khorev is accused of disseminating deliberately falsified information, denigrating both the Soviet State and its social order.

'Khorev has just admitted that he only wrote four of these articles and not all eight. He has also admitted that in his article 'Holy Disobedience' he was indeed calling people to ignore the legislation of 1929, but not with the intention of denigrating the Soviet State or its social order. In its assessment of this article the court has not correctly understood the true viewpoint of the accused. In none of the other articles that he wrote is any mention made of the policy of the government towards this legislation. In the light of this, your Honour, I consider the charge brought against Khorev on the basis of article 203/I as unjustified. Nor have I come across any substantial evidence, either in his articles or in his speeches that were supposedly taped, which would prove that he disseminated fictitious propaganda against the Soviet State. Neither is the charge based on article 143/I substantiated. Might I refer once again to the content of this article: "Any activity, or the leading of any activity, having the semblance of religious ceremony or religious proclamation that causes damage to other citizens' health or in any other way injuriously affects them . . . "

'This article also goes on to mention any activity which encourages others to neglect their communal and civic duties. In my view this charge cannot be substantiated by any evidence presented during this particular court hearing. Have any facts been presented by Khorev's detractors during this court hearing which prove that he organised religious activities which were in any way harmful to the physical health of other citizens? I would like to state most categorically not. Even the incident of 2nd May 1978 in Kizkov forest, where Khorev spoke to the young men eligible for military service, is not conclusive. Also we see that the evidence submitted by the witnesses is contradictory. For example, in his testimony Toake claims that Khorev instigated these young men to refuse military service. But another witness, Babish, on the other hand, testified that Khorev taught them how to behave while they were in the army. So one is led to ask: why should he teach them how to behave during military service if at the same time he is exhorting them to refuse military service? So we see quite clearly that the evidence submitted by these two witnesses is questionable. According to our law, any incidence of questionable evidence always works in favour of the defendant and not the plaintiff and will ameliorate any later sentence.

'And so I maintain that the charge based upon article 143/I is also not substantiated. Finally, your Honour, I would like to comment on the severity of the punishment. As the prosecution has already made clear, this case is of special importance. I am of the opinion that this fact should in no way influence the sentence. On the contrary, if this case is of such great importance, then there is an even greater reason why an objective and impartial verdict should be reached. I would like to urge the judges, aware, as I am, of the awesome responsibility incumbent upon them, not to pronounce the maximum sentence, as is being demanded by the State Prosecutor. A sentence can only be really impartial when it takes into account all the circumstances, not only those which are aggravating, but also those which are mitigating. If the Public Prosecutor is today seeking the maximum possible sentence then he is only looking at the aggravating circumstances. It has been mentioned already that this is not the first conviction of the accused. According to article 38 of the penal code of the MSSR this is an aggravating circumstance.

'But there is also another article in this penal code, and let the court please take note, which says that in passing sentence consideration should be made of the state of health of the defendant. We know that Khorev is a second degree invalid. He also has three young children that need to be looked after. The Public Prosecutor has not given due regard to these mitigating circumstances, otherwise he would never have demanded the maximum penalty. I hope that the court will see these as mitigating circumstances and will apply leniency in passing sentence.

'Also, I consider it inappropriate to overestimate the danger posed by Khorev's crime. Our state is strong enough to withstand any kind of crime. And a guarantee for this is the fact that our judges pass sentences that are just and legal.

'Please permit me, your Honour, to express my hope that in this case too you will, in the name of our republic, pass a sentence which is just according to law, and well substantiated.'

Before the court proceedings were terminated, and before sentence was passed, Mikhail Ivanovich Khorev was allowed to speak once more.

Khorev: Your Honour, I've been summoned to bring the concluding word but I feel physically totally exhausted. I also have a violent headache. Please could I postpone my speech until tomorrow?

Judge: No, I'm afraid you can't. We have to conclude this case today. You've had enough time off during these proceedings.

Khorev: I'm afraid my present state of health doesn't allow me to proceed any further.

Judge: I regret to inform you that this courtroom is booked for another trial tomorrow.

Khorev: But we could meet in another courtroom.

Judge: No, there are no other courtrooms here.

Khorev: I'm very sorry that you refuse my request. So I have no other choice but to summon my strength and bring the concluding word.

I don't want to repeat what I've said already. I can only underline the points I made in my speech at the beginning of this hearing when I answered the charges brought against me point by point.

I've paid great attention to them and the evidence given over the past two days. I would like to point out to all present that the witnesses brought against me have been mainly either state officials or members of the police and auxiliary police. Not one witness has been able to substantiate that any of my behaviour has constituted a breach of the peace. On 1st May 76 and 2nd May 78 no one in Kizkov forest complained. The witnesses merely testified that we were asked to stop our meeting. But none of the witnesses indicated whether the nearby holiday-makers were upset by what the young people sang or said or whether they were listening with interest. Nevertheless we are accused of disturbing working people while they were taking their break. We are also being accused of breaching the peace. And how? By singing religious songs? I would like to point out that there were groups of people all over the forest all celebrating these May holidays in their own various ways. I remember a group of ten people playing a tape recorder and singing a song of Ala Pugachova while others accompanied with instruments. They were singing the refrain ' . . . kings can do anything they want. The destiny of the world lies in their hands . . . ' I thought to myself, 'You should get three years too for breaching the peace. You're drawing enough attention to yourselves. But, no, that would be stupid. No one could call that a crime and no one would get locked up for that.' It's been said over and over again that during these young people's meetings and house meetings we sang religious songs. In a free society and in a free country you can sing whatever you want and in your songs you can praise whoever and whatever you want. I don't see any reason why anyone should be charged with creating a public disturbance.

Furthermore, I've been charged with leading a service in Post Street 88, Kishinev. I led services there several times. But this cannot be constituted as a crime. Whom did we disturb? What public order did we violate? Is it not significant that the neighbours on either side of Post Street 88 never complained? None of them is here giving evidence. Nor did neighbours in Sofiyevka or in Leningrad complain. It's only the police and the auxiliary police who have complained. And let me ask which citizens were disturbed. I'm sincerely convinced that our services never offended anyone. But rather it's these police officials who should be charged with disturbing the peace, our peace, by disrupting our services. We are citizens of this country with the same rights as all other citizens. Surely it can't be regarded as a criminal offence that during a wedding celebration in a tent we used a loud speaker. Four hundred people had been invited to the wedding. It would have been impossible to have addressed them all in a tent and for them to have heard without using a loud speaker. Can we really say that it's a punishable offence to use a loud speaker? And it's equally absurd to accuse us of obtaining this loud speaker from abroad. If the loud speakers produced here in the Soviet Union were strong enough we would have used one of those. I really find it contemptible to have to answer such charges.

Your Honour, I'm deeply convinced that whatever I've done, whatever I've written, whatever I've said, can in no way be construed as a violation of article 203/I of the legal code. This article is concerned with the dissemination of deliberately falsified information. This article is specifically referring to someone who knows that something is a lie and untruth and nevertheless spreads it. When I spread something I am most deeply convinced that it is the truth.

I believe I have in no way expressed any lies when referring to the persecution of Christians which seems to come in waves in this country. Nor can any charge be laid against my activities on the basis of article 143/I because I've not deliberately done anything to violate anyone's rights. I'm afraid that those who evaluated my articles formed opinions which in no way concurred with the facts. I must admit to being totally shocked by their evaluation. For example, they said, 'Khorev writes that the purpose of life is to be found in becoming a citizen of heaven, in following the Lord and serving him with all of your heart.' Now if what I said here is a punishable offence then all other Christians who seek to follow their Lord faithfully on earth, by being obedient and true to their duties as citizens, while at the same time looking forward to their hope of eternal life in heaven, must also be condemned with me.

Moreover, I'm also charged with saying that the Lord is a strict and righteous Judge who will one day judge the righteous and the unrighteous. This is not my teaching but it is general Christian teaching and is being taught all over the world. This is also taught by the Orthodox Church and by the Catholic Church. So shouldn't those in Orthodox churches and Catholic churches also be put behind bars? But you don't do that. I believe firmly and am convinced that one day every person will stand before God and will be judged according to his works, I according to mine and you according to yours. This is what I preach. I've also preached about the imminent return of the Lord Jesus Christ. We're waiting for his return and I have exhorted Christians to prepare themselves for it. As a servant of Christ I am obliged to preach the truth and I will continue to do so at every possible opportunity in the future.

Finally, I'd like to say something with regard to the defence which my lawyer gave. I'd like to thank him for his good word and for the evidence which he produced. Unfortunately, I already know ahead of time what sentence will be passed, a five-year term. I am not so naive as to expect anything less than this. I've also followed very carefully the case put forward by the State Prosecutor who is demanding the maximum penalty. With regard to article 142 he is demanding three years' imprisonment because this is the maximum penalty. With regard to article 203/I he is again demanding the maximum, even though here the lowest penalty is only a fifty rouble fine. Article 203/III has as its lowest penalty a fine, but because I'm a Christian I'll get a three-year sentence. With regard to article 143/I he is definitely arguing for the maximum penalty of five years with the confiscation of property, even though this latter is an optional clause. So I will get the maximum penalty possible.

However, even when I was in the midst of committing this 'crime' I knew what the end result would be. When I first began to follow the Lord I understood fully the import of his words when he said, 'If they persecuted me they will persecute you also,' and I knew that it wouldn't just be a matter of five or more years.

So today I will lose my freedom. I have no regrets because I know I am innocent. But I would like to say quite plainly that the charge against me based on article 142 is just but I am not guilty in this regard. I have disobeyed this article only because the Supreme Soviet of the USSR will one day amend this section of the law governing religious cults, a section which has been in force for more than fifty years and has oppressed all Christians. Of course, if the court were to deliver a verdict of not guilty then I would be overjoyed to be able to go back home with my family. My family and my home mean much to me. But now I tell you, my dear children and my dear wife, that tonight I know I will sleep on a prison bunk.

Since I will never be unfaithful to my Lord I am prepared to go this way. And if my life in exile will glorify him more than serving him in the church then I will rejoice and be thankful to the Lord even for this trial. I have nothing else to say.

A Bouquet of Flowers (a flashback)

I'll never forget the day when I was sentenced for the first time for my service of God. There were many people in the courtroom when sentence was passed. My friends gave me these encouraging words as I set out on this unknown journey: 'God bless you, be strong and be courageous!'

I knew there and then how many years I would be in prison and how old my children would be when I came home. Many thoughts pressed in on me after the trial, but those impressions my friends in the courtroom made upon me are still deeply etched on my memory. What a spiritual freshness and what a joy was to be seen on their faces. They encouraged me and promised to pray for me so that they prepared me to face any difficulty. But the Lord had an even greater comfort in store for me that day.

The police vehicle which we call the 'black raven' was waiting outside. There were already some prisoners in it. Words of greeting were exchanged and flowers were thrown my way. But I had been commanded to walk with my hands behind my back. I tried not to tread on them as I walked but there were so many strewn in my path. My eyes were filled with tears, not because of grief caused by the parting but because of being so deeply moved.

I was the last one to walk between the two rows of policemen to the 'raven' and just before the door slammed shut someone adroitly threw a bouquet of flowers in after me. The prisoners from within the barred off sections of the van grasped after the flowers that had been thrown on the floor and within a short period of time they had all been snatched up. Each one had a flower but the only thing I had was the string which had kept the bouquet of flowers together. Everyone was speaking about his own personal situation and his own impressions of the trial, so no one thought of asking who the flowers were meant for.

Approximately fifteen minutes later the 'raven' reached another one of the court buildings. A young lady aged about twenty-five years old was brought to the vehicle. The men howled like savages and made all sorts of lewd remarks. The woman also had a ready tongue and parried off their remarks with equal coarseness. In the vehicle she was put into one of the so-called 'boxes' in which there was only enough room to sit. Then the usual conversation began, 'What are you in for?' and so on.

Suddenly someone said jokingly, 'Hey, lads, why don't we present our young lady with some flowers?' Everyone quickly handed their flower back through the bars to one of them who collected the bunch together. He then said to one of the guards, 'Please will you give these to the young lady next to us.' The guard obligingly opened her compartment and handed her the bunch of flowers.

She was amazed: 'Hey, fellows, where did you get these beautiful flowers from?'

'We don't know. They were thrown in for someone.'

Then she began to ask each one of us, 'Do these flowers belong to you?' When my turn came I admitted that they belonged to me.

'Well, why don't you have them then?'

'Well, some friends threw them in for me but I didn't manage to catch them.'

'What are you in for? It's funny to be given flowers just after a trial.'

'I was sentenced because I serve the Lord and am a Christian.'

Then a lively conversation ensued. I was asked many questions about the Holy Scriptures. As it turned out the woman had once been put in a cell with a Christian lady. I was very happy to send greetings to this sister in Christ through her.

The young lady stopped swearing and asked, 'What sort of work were you doing in the church?'

'I was an elder.'

Then she asked me, 'Please will you promise to pray for me today. I'm a human being too and I need that salvation your Christian sister was telling me about. I was brought up in a children's home and this is the first time that I've ever heard about God. I want to have eternal life. Tell me, was she telling me the truth when she said that God would forgive all my sins?'

Some of the men began to make fun of us but she said to me through the dividing wall, 'Don't let them put you off. I used to make fun of this too before I understood what it was all about.' Then she added with total seriousness, 'Hey, fellows, please treat this man with special respect and shake his hand for me. I would do it myself if I were able to.'

Then she made what seemed like a passing remark, 'And why this injustice? Why have the flowers been given to me when they belong to him?' She summoned the guard and said to him, 'Please will you give these flowers back to that man!'

'Do you think I'm here just to be at your beck and call?' he answered.

But she insisted. 'If, for once in your life, you want to do something good, then please, I beg you, do this one thing!'

She was so insistent that the guard finally gave in. He opened her door a little, took the flowers and handed them to me through the bars.

They were no longer the beautiful fresh flowers that my brothers and sisters had thrown in to me amongst the throng of other prisoners. I took the string out of my pocket and bound the bouquet together again with loving care.

'Please say a final word,' the young woman asked me.

'May our Lord Jesus Christ, who will save us from all circumstances, always be with you all.' Everyone said, 'Thank you very much.'

In the meantime the 'raven' stopped in front of a solid wall which could only be opened from the inside. The guard rang the bell. An officer opened the door and I walked into Lefortovo prison, sentenced for the first time in my life, and with a bouquet of wilting flowers.

Our names were called out.

'What are you doing with those flowers in this prison?' asked the officer.

'Some friends gave them to me,' I answered.

'You're not allowed to bring flowers in here. Please dispose of them immediately,' he commanded.

So I carefully put the flowers into a nearby municipal wastebin, as one would put them into a vase at home.

This article was first published in Vestnik Istiny, issue no. 4, 1980.

It turned out that Mikhail Ivanovich Khorev was sentenced to five years' imprisonment under strict regime as well as having his property confiscated. During the court proceedings Khorev's wife had to be continually requested not to throw flowers to her husband. Despite all commands to the contrary and hassle from police officers, the young people continued to sing Christian songs and flowers were thrown to Mikhail. The only answer that Khorev could give to these flowers, even to the ones which landed in the police transport vehicle, was to raise his hand in greeting. This was his final farewell to his friends and relatives.

Part Two

'I Write to you, Children . . .'

Mikhail Khorev's prison letters to his children

First Letter   28th January 1980

Many greetings to you, beloved.

I sense an urgent need to comfort you even though I myself, like you, also need to be comforted. Well, here I am again in prison. And here we are separated again. Jesus Christ comforted his disciples at the time of their affliction with the following words, 'My peace I give unto you.' And Christ does give us his peace. Let us worship our Lord for this wonderful gift!

Dearest ones, don't consider yourselves unfortunate when you are afflicted. Don't think of yourselves as orphans now that I have come to prison again for my service of Christ. Christ will give us his peace and this will compensate for any loss we might suffer.

I know that you want to know as much as possible about my situation, and especially about these first days in prison. I sense your disquiet and just want to share with you a few things. But I'll never be able to do this in one letter, so be patient and wait for the following letters also.

I was arrested on 26th January 1980 in Leningrad when I was in the home of a Christian sister. It was half past midnight. Saturday had just begun. Two criminal police, guarding the house and waiting for me (do you remember how our house in Kishinev was guarded around the clock?), took me to the local police station. I was put into solitary confinement for three days. I knew that this arrest was to mark the beginning of my third term of imprisonment.

As soon as they had put me in the cell and bolted the door I began to pray. It was a prayer of thanks. I thanked the Lord for everything: for the path of thorns that Christ walked, as well as for the church which had also followed him for the past twenty centuries. I thanked God that he had granted me to taste not only the joy of salvation but also the joy of suffering for his beloved church. I thanked God for my cell in which I was now taking, by prayer, my first step into the unknown. I also prayed for all of you that you wouldn't grieve over me too sorely, but would commit all of your questionings to the Lord. I prayed that you might wholeheartedly follow him. It was extremely cold in the cell. Despite my winter clothing I froze and so had to keep moving around all the while. Whenever tiredness began to overcome me I would start to do physical exercises until my strength gave out. Then I quickly took off my coat and lay down on the bunk, using my coat as a sheet to lay on as well as a blanket to cover me.

Wrapped up thus I quickly fell asleep until I woke up because of the severe cold. My feet were like blocks of ice. I warmed up again by intense physical exercise but I could not get back to sleep. My strength had been renewed sufficiently by those two hours of sleep.

Sunday. I knew that within a few days I would be taken to the Kresty prison in Leningrad. I waited for this moment with an almost holy reverence. No doubt you will ask why.

When my father was forty-eight years old he too was arrested for his service of God, and brought to this same prison. At that time I was seven years old. Now I myself had become a father and was following the way he had gone through these same prisons, perhaps even through the same cells.

I thought back to my childhood, especially remembering the last talk I had ever had with my father. I was very deeply moved and fell at Jesus' feet, thanking him for my parents who had taught me to love the Lord Jesus more than anything else on earth. How quickly this Sunday seemed to pass. I spent it in singing and praying and in many pleasant memories.

I really would love you, dearest ones, to share in that joy I experienced on Sunday 27th January 1980. Please ask the Lord to smooth the way for me to send you another letter, when I will continue what I have begun to relate to you.

Second Letter

'Remember the way that the Lord has led you' (Deut 8:2).

Dearest ones, today I'd like to carry on from where I left off in my last letter. Yes, that Sunday is impressed in my memory as a glorious time, one on which the Lord was near to me and one on which he reminded me of his wonderful works for me.

I was all alone and there was no one to distract me. I will try, God willing, to relate to you the memories that came back to me on that day, and those lessons I had learned in childhood. My father devoted much time to instructing us in the teaching of the Lord. But here I'd like to concentrate on just one talk that he had with me, one which really moved me deeply as I pondered it alone in my cell.

It was 1938. The church had been going through a very difficult time, and particularly then. We were living in Leningrad and that year all fourteen houses of prayer had been closed, church workers had been arrested and many of their families banished to the north. This was also our fate, because my father held office in one of the Baptist churches in Leningrad. All of those who carried any sort of responsibility or, in some cases, just ordinary church members, were arrested and father too was expecting to be arrested at any moment. He had already packed a rucksack that he left near the door of our room. We children often looked inside the rucksack to see what was in it. He had packed underwear, a black shirt, patched trousers which had wadding in them, felt boots which my father had soled himself, and then a bowl, a spoon and a mug. That was all.

My father's trade was an electrician. One day, after work, he was sitting at his table writing. We children sat down next to him and he began to share with us some things that were deeply etched upon his soul.

'Children,' he began, 'I've got to go on a long journey. I don't know whether I'll ever come back home again. Only the Lord knows the way ahead and he also knows the difficulties that await me along the way and how long my journey will last. And now, as I am about to set out on this long journey, I would like to tell you where we are to meet again, so that we will never be separated again but be with one another for ever.'

To make it clearer for us he explained that whenever you went to a place where there were a lot of people, whether it be a market-place, a large store or a railway station, you always worked out a rendezvous point, just in case you should get separated. You can use different things as rendezvous points, such as the entrance to a market, or the information desk at a station, and so on.

'We will be separated for a short while,' he continued. 'So children, I would like to suggest that we make our rendezvous point at the "white throne". As soon as you reach the heavenly Jerusalem, you will come to a white throne, which Jesus will be sitting on. I'll be there waiting for you. There we will meet up and we will never be separated again.' Then he took his pencil and began to draw this heavenly place and the white throne to which everyone had to come to worship God. There was no undue emotion as he spoke to us, but he described everything in such a totally absorbing manner that there was no way that we could remain indifferent to what he said. My whole life long I will never forget what he told us that evening.

Father knew that he would never again see freedom, but with his usual deep faith he committed his family and himself to the Lord and followed Jesus courageously, knowing that he who suffered with Christ would also reign with him. Besides having this holy reverence and trust himself, father wanted his children to have it too.

Three or four days later he was arrested. We were only allowed to accompany him as far as the door, and no further. The 'black raven' stood outside our window and we could very clearly see father, guarded by the soldiers and with his small rucksack on his shoulder, looking across at us and smiling. Then he raised his right hand in greeting and bade us farewell. That was it. The van door closed and took him away. It was eight months before we received a letter from him, the last letter he wrote, from the far north. He wrote that letter shortly before he went home to be with the Lord, perhaps one or two hours before his death. (In 1955 I met a Christian brother who had been with him at that time. He told me much about my father's last days.) He didn't write much in that letter, simply: 'Dearest ones, when you receive news that I have died, pay no heed, for Scripture says that whoever believes will never die but passes from death into life.' There in my cell, on 27th January 1980, I thanked God for my father and asked God for the strength and wisdom to be a father like him, and leave behind for you, my dearest children, an example of true discipleship.

Five months after father's arrest I was able to see him when I visited him in Kresty Prison in Leningrad. But I will tell you more about this in my next letter.

Third Letter

One evening mother came home and told us that father had been sentenced to five years' imprisonment and that we would be allowed to visit him next day in prison. This was a really special day for us. You know how it feels to visit your father in prison because this is the third time I have been arrested and each time you have been to see me.

What do my childhood memories retain of that visit? I will try to relate everything to you step by step. The prison authorities had told mother that they should not really allow her a meeting with her husband because he was 'propagandising' in his cell. 'But for the sake of your children we will let you meet him.' During the visit my mother asked father, 'They say that you are "propagandising" here!' Father smiled and said, 'Yes, I do pray openly on my knees, and then after praying people ask me questions. So I spend all the days in my cell talking to people about God.'

First of all I would like to tell you about the externals of that visit. Those of us allowed to visit (about fifty of us in all) were led into a large room, and were instructed as to how we should behave during the visit. We were not to talk too loud, nor to hand anything over or touch one another. Then a door was opened and we were allowed into the visiting-room. We children were the first to run in but immediately we got totally lost. The room was done out in a very unusual way. I will try to describe it to you.

The large meeting-room was divided by a U-shaped counter. On one side of the counter stood the prisoners and on the other side the visitors. Prison officials were continually on patrol and keeping watch. There was a large table in the middle of the room.

So we ran in and stopped to look at those standing around. Suddenly we heard a well-known voice: 'Hallo, children!' Then I saw father leaning on his elbows on the counter and smiling. My three sisters and I ran over to him, but the counter was too high for us to reach up to him and so we had to step back in order to see him. Then all the other visitors came into the room and stood two deep along the counter. The grown-ups themselves could hardly see anything, let alone the children, because there was so much commotion in the room. Everyone was trying to talk above the din to make himself heard to the person on the other side. I clambered up on to the table and watched the whole proceedings from there.

To father's right there was a very haggard-looking Jew. Tears were streaming non-stop down his face. He tried to talk to his wife but was very agitated. Then suddenly he yelled out aloud, 'Comrades, please be quiet!' Everyone spoke in hushed tones but then he piped up above them all, 'Firohka, believe me! I am totally innocent!' He wanted to tell his wife something else, but the general noise level increased again and what he had to say was lost in the babble of voices.

The whole atmosphere was most interesting for me. Everyone was very uptight and on both sides of the counter many were weeping. But my father just smiled at us with a twinkle in his eye. From where I was standing on the table I could not hear anything of his conversation with mother. There was a deafening noise going on, but the serenity, peace and hint of rejoicing apparent in my father's demeanour, gaze, and whole behaviour, made a lasting impression on me.

The thirty-minute visit passed very quickly and one by one people reluctantly began to leave. We children were the last ones to leave. Daddy said to us, 'Do you remember where I told you we would meet? At the white throne!' And leaning on his left elbow on the counter he raised his right hand and pointed his index finger into the air. We didn't know that we were saying our last farewell to father forever.

During this meeting he had had very bad pain in his legs, but he didn't tell mother about this so as not to sadden her. It was not until 1955, when I just happened to meet that brother who had been in the same prison as my father, that I discovered he had been in such intense pain that he had not been able to make it to the visiting-room on his own but had had to rely on the help of other prisoners.

That was my first and my last meeting with father while he was in prison, but my childlike consciousness was to be deeply stamped for the rest of my life with the memory of him as a faithful servant of God. Now I want to imitate him also. And I know with great certainty that I will meet him at the white throne in heaven and that when we see one another our joy will last forever.

Fourth Letter

Dearest ones, I am sure that you can still remember the description of my first Sunday in prison. I'd like to carry on now with other memories I have.

I knew that arrestees were transported across to the prison every Tuesday and every Friday. For me this would mean that a 'black raven' would transport me across to Kresty prison on 29th January, exactly forty-two years after my father had gone the same way. Oh, how much I wanted to tell him, 'Father, I will come to the white throne to praise our Lord Jesus Christ the Victor. There I will meet you and all of God's other saints who have trodden the path of thorns that Christ trod.'

But before reaching that glorious destination you must first of all walk the narrow way of prisons, trials, interrogations and long separations. How can a person ever talk about everything that happens to him along life's way!? But these memoirs of mine would be incomplete if I left out an episode of great importance to me.

When father was arrested he suggested that we pray together as a family before he left. I can no longer remember what I prayed or what my mother and sisters prayed, but I do remember what my father prayed: 'Dear Lord, I love my wife and children very much. But more than anything else in the world, Lord, I love you and this is why I have chosen the narrow way of thorns. I commend my family to you, O Lord, with all their needs and requirements, and I am comforted that you always remain faithful to your promises. I know that in the days to come I will see my whole family again before your throne. I praise you for the hope you have given me today. Even as we part I bless your name.'

My dear children, that day I thanked the Lord especially for my parents, who had loved God with all their hearts, minds and souls. I have it on my heart to tell you about this in more detail sometime, but today let me tell you what happened on the Monday, the second day of my imprisonment.

I've already told you how I was put into a cell on my own. The rest of the cells filled up within three days. In the corridor in front of my cell a small table was set up and an older police official took his place at it to take the fingerprints of the prisoners.

This official was very talkative and wanted to know everything. He was really very inquisitive. He asked each one of us why he had been arrested. Sometimes he expressed his sympathy, other times his reproach, as he carried on with his job. He reprimanded two alcoholics, 'You must drink moderately, like I do, and only on special holidays.' He reproached one man for his lack of fatherly feeling because he had neglected paying alimony. He chided a rapist for his part in the general decline of morals. He had something to say to everyone. To hooligans he said one thing, to thieves another. What he was saying so interested me that I listened very attentively and wondered what words of admonition he would have for me.

At last my turn came. My sentence, set by the State Prosecutor, and the charge of violating article 142 of the legislation governing religious cults was read out. The old gentleman looked at me with some astonishment: 'I don't understand what this is all about. Why have you been arrested?' I explained to him briefly that I was a Christian and I preached the gospel to him. I told him about the salvation to be found in Jesus Christ. I spoke for two to three minutes and was not interrupted. Then I asked those listening to me (three people), 'Have you ever read the New Testament?' Instead of answering, the old official asked me, 'What denomination do you belong to?' No sooner did I tell him I was a Baptist than his whole attitude towards me changed dramatically. He started to bawl at me and accuse me of all sorts of awful sins, such as sacrificing children and committing immorality during services, and so on.

He was quite worked up as he took my fingerprints. I then returned to my cell. He, however, could not settle down and continued to speak to me through the locked door. He hurled all manner of insults at me, calling me a traitor, an American agent and a hypocrite. It's not worth mentioning everything he said. He wasn't only referring to me, but to all Christians. His final remark was, 'If it wasn't for you, Communism would have been established long ago.' I wondered why he should have such hatred against Christians and why he should make these terrible accusations. Perhaps, I thought to myself, he knows people who call themselves Christians but are not, and perhaps their behaviour has given him reason to slander the church of Christ. I gently asked him through the door whether he had ever known or talked to any Christians, or whether he had had any Christian neighbours. To my amazement it turned out that he had never met any Christians and this was the first time he had ever seen a Baptist. Yet he seemed to know all about us from second-hand accounts. He had also read a lot and had seen crazy fanatics like me on the cinema screen. Every day he would throw all sorts of false accusations at me, so that eventually I just switched off.

'Pray for those who accuse you,' was one of the things Christ had taught. Now it was up to me to keep this commandment. But whenever that official looked through the spy-hole in my cell door and saw me on my knees he flared up into a terrible rage. How sad it is when folk are so deceived and crippled by sin. And there are so many such people. May the Lord forgive them.

Fifth Letter

It really grieved me to hear such false and undeserved accusations levelled against Christians. It hurt even more to know that they were just taken from anywhere, and expressed by a man who had never known any. He based all these accusations on pure hearsay. But this was nothing new. I often remember 16th May 1966.

The church of Jesus Christ was going through a very hard time. Persecution of Christians was increasing throughout the country. We were being prevented from holding services and were having to pay very heavy and disproportionate fines. Criminal files were being opened on believers and some were arrested, while others were dismissed from their places of work or excluded from places of education. It was significant that all these measures began to be applied throughout the country at the same time. It was very clear that the order to persecute believers had emanated from the top, from Moscow. So the Christians decided to make a personal visit to the Central Committee of the Communist Party of the USSR to raise this matter and, if possible, speak with the chief of the Communist Party, Leonid Brezhnev.

So on 16th May 1966 approximately 450 representatives of the churches of the Evangelical Christian Baptists travelled to Moscow and assembled at ten o'clock on the dot outside the main entrance of the CPSU buildings.

In this letter I can't go into all the details of everything that happened, even though you would like to know them I'm sure. I'll just say that the delegation was not received, even though they had waited for over twenty-four hours in front of the Party (CPSU) buildings. The next day the delegates were bundled into buses and brought to Lefortovo prison. There they were given various sentences, some two to three years' imprisonment, others were just detained for between three and fifteen days. Most of them were transported back home after three days. So this was how the pilgrimage to Moscow ended.

Dear children, perhaps you're wondering where I was during those fateful days. Well, I'll tell you.

On 19th May Georgi Vins and I were commissioned by the Council of Churches and sent to go to the same Party buildings to hand in a petition requesting the release of the delegation which had been sent a few days earlier. We were received by the deputy reception officer, Mr Sklyarov. After listening to our case with great sympathy and showing apparently great amazement at the unjust treatment inflicted by the local officials upon our people, he advised us to get in touch with the Ministry for Internal Affairs. In our presence he telephoned the Ministry and then assured us that we would be received well there. Scarcely, though, had we left the reception room before we were arrested by the KGB and taken immediately to Lefortovo prison.

But my purpose in writing to you today is not just to tell you about my first arrest. I was not one of those delegates who waited on the 16th and 17th May in front of the CPSU buildings although I did witness the event as an uninvolved onlooker like many others there in the centre of Moscow that day. A lot of people were standing round and wondering what these unusual goings-on meant. They witnessed hundreds of people praying on their knees and singing Christian songs. These worshippers were then surrounded by the police. It was an unusual spectacle. Passers-by gathered in small groups of five or ten on the pavement opposite the CPSU buildings. The amazing thing was that in the midst of each group there was a remarkably well informed person who had a pat answer for every question asked by the passers-by. Yes, you're right. These people were police 'plants' or plain-clothes policemen. They smiled pleasantly as they spoke with the curious onlookers and went into lengthy explanations, while all the time keeping their audience under the sharpest scrutiny. I approached several of these groups to hear what was being said about the Christians.

In the first group I approached a police sergeant explained, 'These people are Baptists. They have come from various parts of the country to seek legitimisation for their practices. But judge for yourselves, could our government authorise indecent behaviour which could lead to the moral breakdown of our society?' An old lady asked, 'What sort of indecent behaviour?' The sergeant answered with an embarrassed smile, 'I'm afraid, Ma'am, I can't answer your question with these young people present.' I was horrified when I heard such blatant untruth and approached another group of about ten people. A plain-clothes policeman, about forty years old, was answering their questions.

'You want to know what these Baptists want? Well, they don't like the way we educate our children. They don't let their children go to our schools. In fact, they even forbid them to read books.' And so on. Whichever group I approached, the same lies were being perpetrated. Not one single word of truth was said. I just wished that I'd been able to counter their questions with the truth. Why had these Christian people, old and young, men and women, been forced to come from the furthermost parts of the country to the Communist Party headquarters? Why were they being arrested? By the 'firm' measures adopted against this peaceful delegation on those two awful days, the highest authorities of our land were withdrawing the Christians' rights to even speak about the 'violations' committed in the various parts of the country they had come from. But the church of Christ survived those difficult days by the help of God. She was enabled to look courageously to her future in the knowledge that the Lord would give her the necessary strength to bear any deprivations, arrests or partings from loved ones demanded of her.

I would like to go on to tell you of another incident that happened to me. In the summer of 1979 I was at a service in Rostov. Since the police had already been tipped off that I was coming they turned up during the service, broke up the meeting and arrested me. I was bundled into the back seat of a Volga car and was about to be driven off to the police station. Many people were standing around the car, most of them being neighbours who upon noticing so many police around had come to see what was up. Some of the older women stuck their heads through the open windows and pointing to me, asked, 'What's that man done wrong? These people only pray. They don't do anyone any harm or disturb anyone. Why are you arresting them and taking them off?' The Volga windows were quickly wound up and, instead of answering, the leader of the group which had broken up the service (I forget his name) turned to me and said, 'Just look at how many people have gathered. If we stop and talk with them and tell them the truth about you and your activities, they will tear you to bits if we let you loose amongst them.' And then, with a sardonic smile, he added, 'So, of course, we need to protect you.'

I did not argue with him. I knew from bitter experience how atheistic propagandists have been taught to stir up crowds by spreading the most outrageous lies, leaving the mob baying for blood. But praise God that his Holy Spirit is still with us and saves us from total destruction. God's grace upholds us. Thanks be to God!

Dearest beloved, don't be deflected from the right path, even when your name is dragged through the mud. Rejoice and be glad when this happens because you are being maligned for the sake of Christ. That is a great honour for us.

Sixth Letter

Dear children, in this letter I'd like to fill you in a bit more as to what happened to me on that first Sunday of my third term of imprisonment.

The first two days I spent in the Leningrad police station were not at all alike. Whereas the first Sunday had been a day of thanksgiving, praise and joy, the subsequent Monday was a day of questions and answers for me. That day many undeserved charges and accusations were brought against the church of Christ. I don't wish to repeat everything here, but there are certain questions which came up that really made me think long and hard, and I feel I must make mention of this.

In an earlier letter I've already described to you how I was in a cell on my own and, though it was a bitter experience, my soul was in great need of that time. In the corridor on the other side of the door there was a mighty hullabaloo going on and I heard my name being abused. I knelt down and prayed for these unfortunate people who had been deceived by atheistic propaganda.

A police official opened a small food trap in my cell door (through which food was passed to me during mealtimes) and began to ask me how long I had been a Christian, what sort of family I had grown up in, how many previous convictions I had, why I had been convicted, and so on. Finally a conversation ensued with many others gathering around the door to listen. One person said, 'You must have a lot of money, don't you?' I asked him why he thought this.

'Well, it's your third time in prison for your beliefs and if you voluntarily come, then you must be pretty well-off not to have to live out there in freedom and earn a living. It might well happen that you will never get out of this prison alive, in which case your children must be millionaires.'

I didn't try to dissuade him from this idea because that would have been pointless. But I would like to bring this matter up with you in this letter, beloved.

I became a Christian at the age of seventeen. I made a very conscious act of commitment and my only desire was to be kept in purity and holiness throughout the whole time of my earthly pilgrimage. I didn't choose Christ's narrow path for the riches, fame or comfortable life it would bring, for I had experienced several times in my family before I became a Christian that true discipleship would mean a life of persecution. My father was studying at night school in a local high school, but was forced in 1934 to give up because he was told that there were already enough self-made students around. In 1936 my parents had to surrender their personal ID cards, thus being condemned to an existence on the breadline. My first encounter with real hunger was not the Leningrad blockade of 1941, but actually much earlier. My father went home to his eternal rest in 1939, but his family was left battling on in life (certainly not as millionaires as they did not even have a crust of bread to call their own).

As a child I was often subjected to the scorn and reproach. At school my teacher, a lady, would say time and time again, pointing to me, 'You are the son of an enemy of our people.' That was because my father had been sentenced to five years in prison on the basis of article 58, which dealt with political offenders. I kept quiet. When I came home and told my mother she comforted me as best she could. She would simply say to me over and over again, 'Young man, they said much worse things about our Lord Jesus Christ. Bear it.' And I bore it, and grew up.

When I came of age I chose to go the way of Christ, the narrow way strewn with thorns. Why did I do this? Because I knew that it was only this way that led to eternal life in Jesus Christ.

I remember one evening when the Lord touched my heart in a special way. It was 7th December 1949. The Lord came to me, blessed my heart and placed his Holy Spirit within me. I was exceedingly happy that evening. I still remember what I prayed. 'O Lord God, reign over me as your own possession and make me ready to become an obedient tool in your hand.' Shortly before this I had preached on the text 'Thy rod and thy staff they comfort me'. That message touched me very deeply, even though I was the one giving it. When I was on my own again I continued my prayer, 'Lord, you are my Shepherd forever and I am your sheep forever. May your rod always be in your hand so that when I am in danger, you will protect me from my enemies, or when I stray from your way into wrong paths, either through temptation or through the fear of difficulties, you will use your rod to bring me back to the right way. And should I ever ask you, O Lord, for anything different from what I am asking you now, please ignore it and please let the covenant we are making today be an everlasting one of faithfulness between you, my Lord, and me, your servant.' I uttered this prayer in the stillness and isolation of my secret closet and my Lord, who sees in secret, has and will reward me openly.

In the early years of my youth I could never even have dreamed of serving the Lord in any great way in the church. But it had always been my heartfelt desire to become a preacher of the gospel. And the Lord helped me in that desire. How did it begin? In the church I sought out people who were first-time visitors to our meetings, or those who were on their own and whom no one befriended. These people were mostly students, artisans, soldiers or sailors who happened to stray into our meetings. Then others followed my lead. And so it was, in due course, that a bond of friendship developed amongst us, young people who were of like mind. We sought to grow in our knowledge of the Bible as well as in good deeds. But our first priority was always to preach the good news of the gospel. Really you couldn't call what we did preaching. Rather we talked about our personal experiences with God. But it never even occurred to me to use the preaching of the gospel of salvation as a means of obtaining material gain. On the contrary, I used whatever material gain I had for the preaching of the gospel. Dearly beloved children, does your commitment to the Lord mean that you hold nothing back? Centre all the interests of your life in him and he will bless you. In one of my future letters I will tell you how I became a worker in God's kingdom. May the Lord bless you, beloved, in every good work.

Seventh Letter

Dearest children, as promised, I would like to tell you about my third day in prison. I have already told you how I was expecting a vehicle to come and take me to

Kresty prison on the Tuesday. I was no newcomer to prison life, since I had already been arrested previously. But I had never before been to Kresty prison.

I have already told you how this prison had associations with my childhood. My father had been in Kresty prison in 1938.

'And tomorrow,' I thought to myself, 'I will follow his steps. Perhaps I will even be put in the same cell.' But a guard broke the train of my thinking, as the door was opened and I was summoned to the guard room. Two or three minutes later I was put into the custody of an old and taciturn man. He took up my file and beckoned me to follow him. In front of the entrance was a vehicle. I got into the back seat and a young police sergeant occupied the seat next to me, while the chief of the group got into the front, next to the driver. The vehicle then left.

Where was it going? I knew the city well and paid careful attention to the route we took to keep my bearings. The vehicle drove over the Liteiny bridge. Perhaps they were driving me to the KGB administrative building on the right-hand side. But no, we didn't turn right. We passed the KGB buildings, and then passed Kresty prison. Where were they taking me to then? Everyone was quiet in the vehicle. Not a word was said. Ten minutes later it became very clear that I was being taken to the airport. Then alarm bells rang in my mind. Where were they going to fly me to? I thought of Georgi Vins. He had been flown several times to Moscow before finally being deported to America. I must confess that I became very uneasy. I was prepared in my heart to appear in court and defend the message of Christ. Yes, that is what I desired with all of my heart. But deportation? No, not that. That was not the sphere of service for me, not because witnesses to Christ are not needed in the West, but because my job was to work in the Soviet Union.

During the three days of my imprisonment my mind had become so conditioned to the thought of being a prisoner for our Lord Jesus Christ with a special mission to fulfil that I didn't want anything else at that time. As we drove to the airport I prayed, 'O Lord my God, the point of my life is to glorify you in this world. Therefore take control of me and through me do whatever you deem to be the best for your church and for your glorious name. O Lord, if my imprisonment will bring you more glory than a life spent in freedom then why should I choose freedom? May every day of my time in prison be blessed. O Lord, you are worthy of all honour, glory and majesty. And all over the world, in every country and in every language your name is being praised. And if you, O Lord, have ordained that I bring you more glory in court in the USSR, then why send me to the pulpits of the West? And even if my death should bring you more glory than my life in freedom, then why should I choose freedom? Everything comes from you, O Lord my God, and everything is for you!' These were my prayers and meditations. No one spoke to me as we drove to the airport, and during this forty-minute journey I was lost in deep contemplation. It then became apparent that I was to be flown to Kishinev. Two police officials had been despatched from Kishinev to escort me there.

I was seated in the aeroplane by 6 pm. In the meantime everything had become clear to me. I was going to Kishinev prison, and thus not the one at Kresty. But there were many other prisons awaiting me, transit gaols where prisoners lived in terrible, almost intolerable, conditions that beggared description. All this yet lay before me. In the ensuing letters I will try to portray to you what we had to endure, so that you too can praise God with me for his majesty and for the might he grants at times of particular distress, as well as for his peace and his balm which he grants to those who are exhausted. I'd like to tell you about many, many things, should circumstances permit.

I was seated in the aircraft and out of the window I could see the plane ahead of us making its way to the runway. We were next. It was heading for Moscow, ours for Kishinev, the Moldavian capital.

I thanked my Lord that evening for flying in an aircraft. Anyone who has ever been in prison knows only too well the long journeys prisoners have to endure to get to their prison or labour camp. Instead of spending forty to fifty days being transported from Leningrad to Kishinev, I was making that journey in two hours. This too was an evidence of God's help.

The police official who sat next to me didn't talk the whole time, so I was able to reflect during the entire journey. I thought about the testing before me and then an event came into my mind that had happened twenty years previously. 1960 was the first time I had ever flown from Leningrad to Kishinev. I flew to a youth conference of the Baptist Union which was held in Trusheny, not so far away. It was November, and this was the first conference of its sort in our whole country. This made the present flight to Kishinev even more significant for me because twenty years of Christian ministry were sandwiched between the two. What was I flying into now? I knew the answer: 'I am going to have to give account for the past twenty years of Christian service for the Lord.' May the Lord be with you, my beloved sons.

Eighth Letter

In this letter I would like to tell you about that last visit I was ever to make to Kishinev. During my twenty years of

Christian ministry I had often been there. First of all, in February 1962 we decided to move there from Leningrad. Then while working as an itinerant evangelist for the Council of Churches I was able to get home once a month (sometimes less often). Then again, one of my responsibilities was to work in the Republic of Moldavia, and this meant that I could visit Kishinev more frequently than if I was preaching in Siberia or Central Asia.

So let me tell you about my last visit. I arrived at eight o'clock in the evening on 29th January 1980 under guard. The flight had gone by very quickly. I had been totally engrossed with my thoughts the whole trip. I was looking forward to the opportunity of defending the message of Christ in a city where twenty years previously I had first been able to challenge young people at that Baptist Union Conference. I challenged them not to turn away from the law of God and to resist the godlessness which was creeping into the church. These were my first tentative steps into the preaching ministry, but steps that were to bear fruit in due course.

I was one of the first to be escorted off the plane. A Volga was parked not far away. Once again I got into the back seat (as I had done three hours previously in Leningrad) and we set off. It was a quiet evening with good visibility. I knew that I would shortly be able to see my house, since the road we were on went right past it. Our vehicle stopped at a traffic light. No one was on the street. At that time I didn't know that you had just had a house search. It was already your sixth—quite a few. At a later time I'd like to tell you more about house searches. But in this letter I'll tell you what I felt as we drove from the airport to the prison.

As I turned to catch my last glimpse of my house I became very heavy of heart. Why? I reflected. Because I love my family very dearly. I love you all, dear ones. My love for you all is deep and full. I know I don't need to write this but I will do so, anyway, because I want to tell you the truth the way it is. Thank you all for returning my love. But let me add this, that I love the Lord even more and that is the reason why I left home to enter his service fully and completely as an evangelist. Oh, how often I wanted to visit you at home during those twenty years of Christian ministry, just to be with you. But it wasn't my right to decide. Judge for yourself: could I desert my service for Christ just because I wanted to be with my family? I had to withstand many temptations and I would never have been able to remain so steadfast had you not helped me.

I often think back to the day of my ordination at the beginning of my Christian ministry. It was on 14th July 1962 that brothers G A Rudenko and G K Kryuchkov laid their hands upon me and set me aside to the work as an evangelist.[8] Then my wife, who was standing three or four feet away from me, was asked the question, 'Sister Vera, are you agreed that your husband belongs first of all to God, then to the church and only thirdly to you?' I looked at her and didn't know what she would answer. I knew that she would answer positively because I did not doubt that she loved the Lord more than anything else in the world. But how she would answer that was the issue. What words would she use to register her assent? These things I didn't know. One thing was clear to me. The question was a fundamental one and the answer would have to be very deeply considered and binding. All eyes were upon her as everyone waited. She was so choked with emotion that she couldn't utter a word. She simply nodded her head as a sign of agreement, while tears coursed down her cheeks. Then the brother continued, 'Brothers and sisters! Our sister is prepared to surrender her husband to full-time service. Dear sister, we understand the emotional turmoil you are in deep in your soul.

It will be hard for you, but the Lord will be with you. He receives your sacrifice and you will be blessed and rewarded for it, and will see much fruit. May the Lord give you grace. May the Lord help you to be a good companion to your husband.' The most important thing on that day was our joint surrender to the service of our Lord. And I have felt your mother's support during the whole time of my service for him.

Yes, there are many things I could tell you about these twenty years of Christian service, and it is my responsibility to do so. Why? Because your life and mine has been so different from those of others who have lived around us. Other children have been able to spend every day with their fathers, but not you. I was travelling all the while, but even when I came home I could not give you much attention. You know that full well. I can remember how once I promised to spend an evening with you but then Christian brothers visited me with an urgent request and I wasn't able to do it. Your mother said, 'Just don't promise them anything, otherwise later on they won't believe anything you say. They are just not of the age to understand why you haven't got time.' Yes, I have always prayed, and still pray, 'O Lord, might your presence make up to my family the loss they have sensed by my absence.' Since a very young age you have visited prisons to spend a little time with me and bring me parcels. Through your childhood you have learned to write letters to me while I was in prison. Those letters are a continual source of encouragement to me.

As the vehicle stood at the traffic lights near my house I looked along the deserted street, so well known to me, and saw my beloved home, so dear to my heart. Then I said to the Lord, 'O Lord, I have left everything to follow you. Bless my wife, my children, the church which so badly needs able ministers. O Lord, might you call my children into your service.' These were my thoughts as we waited at those traffic lights.

Ninth Letter

Beloved children, I would like to carry on the train of thought begun in my last letter.

I knew that I had been flown to Kishinev to appear in court as a Christian. Once more it was to be my duty to defend God's truth from the defendant's bench, so I had no time for regrets. I have always thanked God for bestowing on me the great honour of following and serving him.

The apostles left everything to follow Christ, and so Peter's question is quite understandable: 'Lord, we have left everything to follow you. What will be our reward?' Jesus didn't regard this as a superfluous question or an immodest request. He didn't say to them, 'You don't know what you are asking!' All followers of Christ must know what they are getting into and why they are to forsake all. Christ told them that those who follow him will receive a hundredfold reward here on earth, and in heaven eternal life.

Dearest children, in this letter I don't want to tell you about earthly or heavenly rewards (even though that would be a fine theme to pursue) but I would like to ponder awhile the first part of Peter's question, 'We have left everything to follow you.'

One time you asked me whether I have found it difficult to forsake all to follow Christ. Yes, I have. As a young man I surrendered my life to the Lord, and as I have already said, my ordination to his service followed in 1962. In the period of time subsequent to this I more than once thought I would never be able to cope with the enormous call upon my spiritual and physical resources.

I won't bother to enumerate here all the times I was hauled out of services to appear at police stations, or to pay fines, or all the times I was in danger. Nor will I tell you about all those who have caused me real heartache in my Christian ministry. I will leave these things, and concentrate in some detail on one event, about which you know nothing.

My journeys often brought me into the regions of Siberia and Central Asia. During the years of 1963 and 1964 I was almost invariably accompanied by a Christian brother, Pavel Frolovich Sakharov (a wonderful servant of God who in the meantime has gone to be with the Lord).[9] In March 1964 we were both in Lvov at a church workers' conference. The next day we were due to be in Kiev and thereafter to leave for Siberia again. Pavel Frolovich said to me, 'Since you are so near to home, why don't you go and visit your family for two or three days? We'll meet up again in Kiev and travel on from there.'

I was delighted at this suggestion and arrived in Kishinev the following day. As I came up the stairs I heard a loud sound of children crying and became concerned because it seemed to be coming from our house. I hastened to the apartment door and unlocked it, while from the inside I could hear the sound of children weeping disconsolately. I pushed the door open and saw your mother, Vera, lying on the corridor floor. Vanyusha was standing near her and howling, while Pavlik was howling almost as loudly from his little bed. At first I didn't ask what had happened but helped your mother to get to bed and settled the two boys. The children were starving hungry and had asked for food. Vera had then had a bad attack, perhaps caused by a liver malfunction (or some other defective organ). She was in no fit state to stand and cook, but since there was no other solution she dragged herself to the kitchen.

I then pitched in and helped, by shopping, cooking porridge and doing some washing.

That same evening there was to be a service in our church. I hesitated a moment as to whether to go or stay at home and help where I was needed.

'The church will really be glad to see you,' your mother said. 'Just leave everything and go to the church. I have no right to hold you back when the church needs you.'

These words touched me very deeply.

The next day she was feeling somewhat better. She got out of bed but still felt very weak. When she discovered that I would have to leave again on Friday and would be away for a long time, she said, 'Isn't our Lord just wonderful!? He sends help at the most needed, critical moment, at the time when you think you have no strength left to bear the cross!'

We thanked God in prayer for her healing, for the help that he had given, and for being together again, and I got ready for my journey. We had had two whole days together. I thought, 'Is it really the right thing to go away for a long time and leave my sick wife with her small children?' I shared my hesitations with Vera and she answered, 'Do you remember the question the brothers asked me during your ordination service? First of all you belong to God, then you belong to the church and finally you belong to our family.' And so it came to a fresh parting, but we both received it with joy.

Perhaps you ask the question why there was no one in our church who could help our family when the church was full of so many good people. And that is true. So many did help, thank God. But let me tell you about another difficulty which I have never shared with you before.

There are not many who can forsake all and devote themselves fully to full-time Christian ministry. In this particular matter we encountered a lot of misunderstanding, or at best only limited understanding as a family. When unbelievers discovered that I was often away they would say to your mother, 'We really feel sorry for you. Why don't you divorce him if he won't help you bring up the children?' I don't mind so much when such misunderstanding comes from unbelievers, because they can't understand what service of God means. But a lot of misunderstanding and contrary opinion also came from Christians.

'Why is your husband off on ministry again when your family needs him so badly back here?'

'It says in Scripture: "If someone doesn't take care of his own family he has denied the faith and is worse than an unbeliever" (1 Tim 5:8). Brother Mikhail knows this passage of Scripture so why is he away so much?'

'Sister Vera, my husband is not like yours. If he sees I am feeling a bit poorly, he will not leave me on my own but will do all the housework himself. But your husband . . . '

'Vera, dear, is the only reason you got married to sit alone at home the whole time?' And so on, and so on.

Dearest children, I don't want to mention other things that were said, although I could write a lot more. It has no profit to do so. Each one judges according to the level of his spiritual maturity. Much also depends upon the goals we have set ourselves in life. The reason I am writing this to you is to awaken within you a spirit of gratitude towards God, gratitude for giving us all the strength needed to endure everything and not to forsake his service.

I would like to make a suggestion to you, beloved, or rather ask something of you. As you reflect on all that has happened in the past, spend an evening offering up prayers of thanks to God (especially before Vanyusha goes into the army). Encourage your mother from Scripture, and above all rid yourselves of everything that hinders your prayer life. Ask one another's forgiveness if there have been any upsets or disputes, and then write to me and tell me all about that evening.

Perhaps you will reply that you don't have enough time. I know that. But forget everything else and do it today, as it is very important. I believe that the Lord will bless your lives very richly. So I should like to close here for today. Sometime later I'll tell you more about our Christian ministry.

PS. Three days have passed since I wrote this letter, and as I have reread it I have hesitated in sending it to you. Is it really the right thing to do to tell your children about difficulties you have encountered? Will they understand? Won't they stand in judgement over those who have misunderstood my service for God and the state my family has been in? After reflecting further, I have decided to send this letter to you after all, but I would like to stress that you should not judge people prematurely. The incidents related mark the very beginning of our service for God. Our Christian friends had become so accustomed to being beaten into submission by this or that Party directive that initially they regarded this mighty movement of God's Spirit with great mistrust.

In my following letters I will elaborate on these things so that you and those of your age can give God the praise and glory.

Tenth Letter

Beloved children, I greet you with the love of God whom I have served with all of my heart from my youth.

I would like to elaborate further on the way that God has led me. I have already written to you that I was flown to the prison in Kishinev. At ten o'clock in the evening we arrived at the gate. When we rang the bell, the guard opened it. Once more I stepped across that well-known threshold, because I had spent a period of time in that prison after my previous arrest. I was searched and put into one of the cells on the second floor. There were two of us in the cell.

Let me tell you about that first evening in this new cell. I was totally at peace since I had commended my way to the Lord. There was only one thing that preoccupied me, namely the defence of the cause of Christ I was to make from the dock. This is what my Christian ministry is all about, really. So this was now my third term of imprisonment and perhaps my last one. Should this be the case, then might the name of the Lord be praised. It is a blessed lot for a Christian to go to be with the Lord while lying on a prison bunk. But one does not always think this way because naturally you want to live—but you also want to fulfil the whole will of God, so you are torn.

One time you asked me why I seemed to have been in prison more than other Christian workers. The answer is simply this: firstly there are others who have been in prison longer than I have. Secondly, God does not allow each one of us to go the same way, or to do the same service. The most important thing for us is not to flinch from suffering for the name of our Lord. I was always afraid of violating God's will. But God is judge of all.

There are some servants of Christ who are totally dedicated to the Lord whose circumstances are different from mine. God is sovereign in all things.

I have had many temptations in my lifetime, and perhaps one of the most difficult of all was the time I had the chance of escaping a prison term and taking up a peaceful ministry for God in the church instead.

For example, on 19th May 1966, when Georgi Vins and I were arrested and held prisoner in Lefortovo prison in Moscow, I was summoned on the fourteenth day of our detention to appear before the examining magistrate. There was another man in his office who was unknown to me and he was to 'decide' our fate. He categorically refused to reveal his name or rank. He asked me what I would do and where I would go if I were set at liberty that day. It became clear to me immediately what they were wanting me to say, which was, 'Of course, I will go home, because I have a wife and small children.' But no! I decided otherwise. My dearly beloved children, I don't know how you will take this. Nevertheless I refused all their offers. I remember coming back to my cell after this interview and sinking down on to my knees, praying, 'O Lord, the Devil tempted you too with all sorts of attractive even seemingly harmless and useful propositions, but you rejected everything. If it is your will for me to go home and for my service to take a different tack, then I am ready for anything. But there is no way I will strike a bargain with the enemies of your church, I cannot do that.' So I chose rather to suffer with the people of God. And from that day on I have been through many different prisons.

Often in life I've had to make a 'yes' or 'no' choice. For example, at special youth meetings during holiday times. I knew full well that anyone who organised such events would be liable to court action but I never sought to shove the responsibility on to anyone else. Why should I have the right to stand on the side-lines and save myself? I did not. So, I appeared in court three times accused of organising youth meetings.

Very often people say that you must protect the servants of the church. And that is true. But a servant doesn't have the right to protect himself for fear of persecution. In the New Testament the Christians wept and sought to persuade the apostle Paul not to go to a town that was potentially dangerous for him. But he refused and would not listen to their persuasion. 'Why do you break my heart?' he said. But we must try to understand these Christians. They loved their apostle and that was a very good sign. But the true shepherd doesn't run away when danger approaches, but rather gives his life for the flock which has been entrusted to him.

One time you asked me whether I'd ever faltered or failed in my service of God so as to escape fresh suffering. The whole of life is a battle. I have had many temptations. But above all I have always sought with the help of God to win the victory over myself. And I thank God for the way I've gone and for the help he has given me.

Eleventh Letter

Beloved children, I am really happy to write to you today because I want to tell you about the trial that took place in Kishinev in April 1980.

This was already the third trial I'd experienced in my life but the day before I was as keyed up as if it were my first. I knew the date of the proceedings a week ahead of time and was able to picture in my mind who would come and what I would say in defence of God's cause and so on. I knew I would be sentenced to five years' labour camp with strict regime and this would be on the basis of four articles of the law. This had been mentioned in the indictment against me. Of course the indictment also contained much that was fabricated, and much that was plainly ridiculous. Surely anyone in their right mind would know full well that no Soviet laws were broken when brother Misha and sister Ruta got married in Chuchelny.

'But this is why we're having the trial, to find out!' the examining magistrate said with a smile. 'We will have the last word! And you will be sentenced to five years in labour camps in the far north.'

I won't bother to dwell on the accusations made against me in the indictment. Rather I would like to tell you about an incident which you yourselves witnessed.

I have always been involved in youth work especially when we had large youth meetings. Even though I knew that my very presence at such events could be construed as a criminal offence, and that I would definitely be accused of organising these events, I nevertheless always sought to be present and take part in them. Moreover, I didn't want to put others at risk and so never shrank from taking on the leadership of such youth meetings. I knew that these meetings would come to the notice of the authorities and I did not want to put another brother at risk by remaining in the background myself.

Many young people would come to these meetings and perhaps hear about the Lord for the first time. Many of them might have already heard the gospel but never surrendered their hearts to the Lord. During these gatherings, many mishaps occur, as happened, for example, on 2nd May 1979. So the leaders of such meetings always bear a great responsibility, not only before God but also before the church and people who come in from outside. Often those who come from the outside don't like these meetings and that's why I was charged according to all four articles of the law.

After all the evidence has been gathered against an accused person, he is informed of that evidence and allowed to appeal against any charge in the indictment. At the beginning of April I was reading the two-volumed indictment brought against me, prepared by Mr Zurkan who was the examining magistrate for specially serious cases.

You can imagine my great astonishment when I perceived from the protocol that all the witnesses summoned to give evidence (over thirty of them) were either police officials, auxiliary police or police informers sent to spy on our services.

One of the inhabitants of the village of Kizkany testified as follows: 'On 2nd May 1979 I was driving with colleagues in a forest when I saw Christians singing, praying and playing musical instruments. A religious banner had been suspended between two trees, while someone was preaching and someone else was reciting poetry. There were between 400 and 500 people present. Those in my party had brought a ball with them and so we played ball near them. I was simply amazed when, after kicking the ball to some of the children and young people in the group, hoping they would play, one of their young boys aged between ten and twelve picked up the ball, brought it back to us, lay it on the floor and then went back to rejoin the others.' So this witness was simply amazed that he could not distract the children from the service and that the boys didn't want to play ball with them. The examining magistrate who heard many other similar testimonies laid the blame fully upon me as the leader of that meeting.

When I read this I was exultant. Thank God for our youth who have from early childhood had the opportunity of seeing for themselves the lamentable behaviour of atheists and have tasted in school the bitter experience of being falsely accused for the name of Christ. You too, my beloved, have experienced much of this in your own lifetime.

Yes, I was the leader of that blessed meeting at which several dozen people (mainly young ones) gave their hearts to God and received forgiveness of sins. During it a notecripted that week. I opened the New word of exhortatn. Then another elder gave them a text to take with themd we prayed for them. That was all that happened.

But the State Prosecutor needed more than that and was after incriminating material. The 'witnesses', police officials and their collaborators, went on to testify, 'Khorev called upon these young men to refuse to bear arms!' The 'witnesses' who had been driven out into the woods to disturb our meetings also confirmed this. Interestingly enough, these witnesses were also those same 'holiday-makers' who had come into the woods for recreation and had been disturbed by the Christians' meeting!

I asked the examining officer, 'How could your collaborators have heard what was said to these young men? Firstly, we didn't have a microphone so that even those standing at the back of the meeting couldn't hear anything, let alone those who were a hundred metres away playing ball or drinking alcohol. Anyway, the main thing is that I didn't say anything at all about refusing military service. We simply blessed these young men by praying for them and then we gave them texts to bless them from the New Testament.'

'The court will examine the matter further,' answered the examining magistrate.

After this cross-examination I invoked my right of appeal and requested that some Christian brothers, who could clarify these matters, give evidence.

A few days later I was summoned and told that my request had been refused. You see, they really needed this part of the indictment so that they could sentence me to five years. I requested again but my right of appeal was absolutely refused.

Once, during a personal interview, the examining magistrate asked me, 'What did you actually say to these boys?' I answered briefly, 'I encouraged them to lead an exemplary Christian life wherever they went, to always make time to cultivate their prayer life and always to carry the Holy Scriptures with them.' I wanted to say more but the examining magistrate interrupted me. 'The indictment is quite just, then! This exhortation alone is enough to get you five years . . . '

Twelfth Letter

Dear children, today I'd like to tell you more about the wonderful deeds of God in my life and how he has led me.

In my last letters I told you something about what happened to me in prison while I was awaiting trial. This day soon came, a joyful day in my life but one which carried a great responsibility with it.

The main thing for me to do that day was to defend boldly the truth of Christ from the dock, as well as to encourage my family and the church which I so dearly loved. Finally, I needed to make my detractors in these court proceedings see that it was not so much the servants of God who were being judged that day but rather Christ himself in his servants.

So eventually the long awaited day arrived. Why do I describe it that way? Well, because the period of cross-examination had wearied me so much that I was looking forward to getting to a camp where at least I would be able to get some fresh air, and visits from my relatives, even though they might not be frequent. Perhaps I might get one personal visit a year and two general visits, lasting for two hours each. During these general visits you speak to one another through two thick panes of glass using a microphone. This of course is very difficult for me with my bad eyesight. But at least there is contact with your loved ones. Besides all this, one is allowed to write two letters a month from the camp, thank God!

I wasn't brought to the court hearing through the normal channels. Usually the accused are kept in box-like containers until they have all been assembled. Then these containers are loaded into the 'black raven' and brought to the court buildings under police escort.

This is the normal way for prisoners to come to court, but not for me. As soon as I was led to the 'gate' cell (the one nearest the prison exit) I was immediately surrounded by police, soldiers and other officers. They already knew who I was and why I was appearing in court. Among them were some of those who had broken up our services. Of course, I could not remember who they were, but they remembered me.

While the barber cut my hair, I overheard the police officials conversing with each other. 'We were once sent to break up these Christian meetings,' one of them said. 'They were getting together on Sunday as usual. It was the first time I'd been at one of their meetings. They were all singing and one of them got up to preach. We told them to break up but they just knelt down and prayed. It would have been easier for me if these people had been drunk and had had a punch-up with us, or had offered some kind of physical resistance. But you just don't know how to handle these people. I only went to one of their meetings and I'd be happy never to go again.' I naturally joined in and told them all I could about the Lord.

Then ten soldiers escorted me to a waiting car. The journey was a short one. The court was convened in a factory clubhouse in Kishinev. I was instructed not to look around as I walked and to keep my hands behind my back, otherwise I would be handcuffed. As soon as I got out of the car I looked around to see if any of my family was there. But there were only strangers who had been brought specially in for this hearing. 'Thank the Lord,' I thought, 'these people will hear the Word of God, and if they don't get saved, at least they'll hear my testimony!'

As I was walking towards the door I heard someone call out, 'Mikhail Ivanovich!' I couldn't recognise the person waving to me because of the distance. 'Thank the Lord,' I thought, 'it is not a secret trial like the last one.' I walked into the courtroom. There were a lot of people there, but no one from my family. So the trial began without you being present, dear ones. The judged asked if I was satisfied with the composition of the court.

'Yes,' I answered, 'but why are none of my family or friends present?'

The judge assured me that they would be permitted into the courtroom for the whole trial but first of all the proceedings had to be opened.

Then there were the usual formalities. I was offered a defence lawyer. 'I am a Christian and am being tried for my service of God,' I said. 'The defence lawyer you are offering me is an atheist. How could he ever understand my point of view? I would be happy to accept a Christian defence lawyer.' My request for a Christian defence lawyer was rejected by the court. They offered me instead a lawyer I had never met before. The judge called for a two-hour recess, so I could get to know the lady lawyer.

And then you came into the courtroom, beloved. When I saw you I knew immediately that you weren't happy with the assigned defence lawyer, especially since a Christian lawyer from West Germany was prepared to defend me. But he was not granted permission.

I will carry on with this subject in my next letter. The Lord be with you.

Thirteenth Letter

Beloved children, has there been a day in your life when you've known that you were standing at a dividing of the way and that the whole of your future depended upon the decision you were to make?

The 7th December 1949 was just such a day for me. It was the day I surrendered my heart to the Lord and he became my God. More than thirty years have passed since that day but the covenant between us is indissoluble. As I was standing there in court I didn't have to make a decision nor did I have to think about what to say. I had already made my decision and that decision had determined the future course of my life. In court I didn't seek to defend myself. It was as if I didn't exist. The whole content of my words was towards defending the proclamation of the gospel in an atheistic country.

As I've already written, the judge decided to give me two hours to get to know my defence lawyer. I was led under guard to the place where I could get to know her.

My defence lawyer was a woman and this lady was a good person. But she understood absolutely nothing about the Christian life. This was the first time in her whole career (and she was already well advanced in years) that she had met such a defendant as myself.

'First of all, I would like to tell you that I plead not guilty,' I said. And then I explained to her that any Christian wanting to serve his Lord faithfully would never be able to abide by the legislation of 1929, since certain clauses in this legislation were specifically aimed against Christians. In fact, this legislation causes all Christians to become law-breakers. To promise to abide by this legislation, so inimical to God, would mean forsaking the gospel and turning away from God's law. This is why Christians have a choice to make, either to trade in their loyalty to God for freedom from persecution, or to remain true to Christ and consequently run the risk of persecution.

I myself had chosen the second course of action because the whole question of eternal life was a central issue for me. Furthermore, as a servant of Christ I was obliged to warn God's people of impending danger. I spoke about this at various preachers' conferences as well as at numerous church meetings. I taught them all to obey and respect authority but wherever this atheistic authority impinged upon our worship of God (in whom it does not believe) then we had to be courageous enough to disobey this authority regardless of the consequences.

'I also plead not guilty to the charges brought against me on the basis of these very articles of the 1929 legislation,' I explained to the lawyer. 'According to article 191 I am accused of resisting the organs of state. But I am not guilty in this regard. This charge is based solely and simply on the fact that I continued to preach after being told to stop by the police officials who came in to break up our peaceful services. By invoking Article 143 they are sentencing me to five years' imprisonment. But I have not violated one jot or tittle of this article even though their "experts" are of the opinion that my articles in *Vestnik Istiny* constitute a violation of other people's peace, because in them I speak about the judgement of God as well as about our glorious hope of heavenly life, about the forgiveness of sins, new birth, and living a holy life in Christ. Yes, I did write this and I have proclaimed the teaching of Jesus Christ. This is my whole reason for living. But if this activity is outlawed by paragraph 143 of the state legislation of the MSSR and if this is my crime, then I count it my good fortune to be thus accused. To use the words of the apostle Paul: " . . . Woe to me if I do not preach the gospel!" (1 Cor. 9:16).'

My lawyer insisted that although there was no way that my personal convictions could prevent me violating Article 143, I should still plead not guilty. We just didn't have enough time to talk it through in detail because two hours were insufficient.

When I came back into the courtroom I was confronted by a wonderful sight. Part of the courtroom was taken up by Christians. I saw my friends, co-workers in the kingdom of God, and my whole family. I wasn't allowed to turn around and face them but nevertheless I managed to see some of them and was strengthened in my morale. I was especially glad that now at last my three sons were able to be eye-witnesses of this legalised persecution of their father. During my two earlier trials in 1966 and 1970 you were not of age to understand everything and draw the right conclusions. But now this was a wonderful day for me. I didn't really think about myself nor did I fear for myself. I was neither intimidated by the thought of the long-term imprisonment nor by the thought of the long and weary passage through various transit prisons.

I long that as you see me and many others of God's workers being tried for their faith in God, you too might fall in love with this persecuted Christ and with his storm-tossed and persecuted church which is 'as powerful as an army' (Song 6:4).

It is a great honour to be rejected by the world and be unjustly sentenced as a servant of God. The words of Christ become very special to me: 'Rejoice and be glad, for great is your reward in heaven' (Matt. 5:12). You can judge whether or not I am succeeding in communicating this joy to you because you yourselves were there on both days and heard everything for yourselves.

The Lord be with you.

Fourteenth Letter

' . . . *So choose today whom you will serve* . . . ' *(Josh. 24:15).*

My beloved children, it is no mere accident that I have headed this letter with the text 'so choose today whom you will serve . . . ' It is very important to make the right decisions in life. If we surrender our hearts and our lives to the Lord and serve him with all of our hearts, he will help us in all the circumstances we will find ourselves in.

I certainly experienced God's help during that trial. You had heard a lot about trials against Christians but it was a new experience for you to witness one first-hand. You heard every word that I said and perhaps after the trial you might have talked among yourselves as to whether I'd done the right thing and set a good example for you or not. My beloved, that's up to you to decide since you heard everything. I must say that I would really rejoice if you became protagonists of the gospel of Christ. May the Lord help you to become such. There is one thing I desire, and that is that you should consecrate your lives to God and with each new day serve him faithfully in all things and with all of your strength.

I really had to gear myself up for the second day of the trial. I had to give my final defence. You know that I never make notes, not even when preaching, because my sight doesn't permit me. So I had to impress everything on my mind and learn it off by heart. I hardly slept that night. It wasn't because I was worried about the future, for on the contrary I was at great peace about it. But I couldn't get to sleep. Many memories were going through my mind and by morning I had a terrible headache.

That's nothing new for me because I nearly always have a headache. At home sometimes I would have such violent headaches that I couldn't speak or turn my head. These headaches were brought on through over-exertion. Then I would go to bed and lie down completely still with closed eyes for two or three hours until they passed. Because of these headaches I had asked for the trial to be postponed until the following day, but the judge refused. I was amazed that I was not only denied the medical help I urgently needed but they did not even offer me anything for these headaches. But on reflection I should not have been amazed since my physical condition suited very well the purposes of my detractors. For not only could I hardly speak but I was barely able to appear in court. I had to summon nearly all my strength to say even a few words in defence of the holy gospel. I do not know how I managed it. It was only with great difficulty that I could remember the next day what I'd said, even though I had recovered from my headache. But I'm not too concerned about that, since I know that you understood correctly what I had to say.

Had I been feeling myself, I would have said the following in my summing up speech: 'My Lord Judge! The whole of my life has been devoted to the service of my Lord Jesus Christ. Today you are sentencing me the same way as my Lord and Teacher Jesus Christ was when he was on earth, in the same way too as the apostles, and most of them were tortured to death. All Christians in every age have been persecuted, some being burned at the stake, others languishing in prisons. But they have handed down the truth of Christ to us in this present age. I am thankful that more recently our fathers too have set us a good example and have remained faithful to God, even to death. My own father trod this path too.

'Here in this courtroom an unusual trial is taking place. In the lives of his modern-day disciples, Jesus Christ is himself being sentenced again. During the court proceedings against me I have not been charged with physical violence or with theft. The only charge brought against me has been that I serve God, preach Christ, and found new churches where previously there were none. And I have indeed done all of that. This is the third time now that I have stood trial. Each time the charges against me have been the same. If suddenly the improbable were to happen and I were to be set free I would be delighted to be able to return to my wife, children and home church. But I would use my freedom to serve my God with even greater zeal. I would continue to exhort all Christians to stick to the truth as delivered by Christ, even though that is why I am being sentenced today. I would continue to instruct young people and children in the teaching and admonishment of the Lord, even though this is what I'm being charged with at this particular trial. And I will continue to do this, not because I am stubborn or find it difficult to learn, or because it means financial gain for me, not at all. I will continue to do it because I am a servant of God and can do no other.'

At the earliest possible opportunity I will continue this letter. Beloved children, remain true to God always and in everything.

Fifteenth Letter

Beloved children, whenever I write to you my heart beats a little faster, as it does today.

I began to tell you something about my life but I don't know whether I can share everything I want to. I'm not so concerned with the literary or stylistic merits of my writings but rather that these words which come deep from within my heart as a father should touch your hearts. I know that my efforts to make Jesus the Crucified, Jesus the Resurrected and Exalted the most precious thing in your life will not be in vain, and this is a comfort to me.

No matter how the storms of life batter this vessel of mine it will remain at peace, even in the most violent of tempests. And the Lord will guide this vessel of mine into his peaceful harbour. But I don't want to arrive there on my own—I want you to be with me, beloved. That peaceful haven of rest is still far ahead of us. The purpose of my life (and I hope the purpose of yours) is to remain faithful to the Lord.

You asked me to describe in detail how the trial went. I will gladly do this. You yourselves were there, so you can get a deeper insight into my side of things. I won't bother to repeat what you saw and heard, nor will I dwell on the prejudice of the examining authorities and the Prosecutor who brought this indictment against me.

But let me talk today about those articles that I wrote, six of which were handed over for scientific and judicial assessment. The assessors, Professor Voronzov, a doctor of historical science, and Mr Andrianov, a lecturer in historical science, were from Leningrad.

I wanted to make a copy of this 'scientific assessment' but the examining magistrate strictly forbade me. It was an extremely interesting document and exposed the rank ugliness of atheism. I did make a note of some of the things in the written assessment and I quote them here.

Question: 'Does the article written by the accused, M I Khorev, in any way encourage citizens to withdraw from social involvement or abstain from their civic duties?'

The question was put in such a way that, should the assessors answer in the affirmative, I could be sentenced to five years' imprisonment under article 143. (Apparently article 142 was not, on its own, enough for the State Prosecutor dealing with the violation of the legislation concerning religious cults.) When the examining magistrate informed me, before the 'scientific assessment' took place, of the nature of the questions, I knew that I would be sentenced to five years. And what was the assessors' verdict? They confirmed 'scientifically' that this was indeed what my article was saying. They wrote, 'M I Khorev sees the ideal Christian as a citizen of heaven. In his article "Christmas Prophecy" (*Vestnik Istiny* no. 4, 1977) he writes, "Since coming to know Christ as Mighty God and Father of Eternity I can testify that I have eternal life and am a citizen of the New Jerusalem, citizen of heaven".'

The following was used in the indictment against me, ' . . . M I Khorev expresses thoughts calculated to intimidate believers by conjuring up the terrible spectre of judgement if they do not fully turn from this world.' To back this accusation up they quoted my words, 'And if you do not receive Christ who has come into this world with the sole purpose of saving you, then I must testify to you that this prophecy will be fulfilled in your life on the day of judgement, not for your salvation but for your judgement, because you did not believe in the name of the only begotten Son of God.'

'Furthermore,' commented the assessors, 'M I Khorev forces these views upon his readers in his article entitled "Envy" (*Vestnik Istiny*, nos. 2–3, 1977). In this article he writes, "If we do not strive to purify ourselves from every defilement of the flesh and spirit then we will have no part in God's eternal dwelling . . . Let us not deceive ourselves." And then, "Nothing impure will ever enter in to the "New Jerusalem" ' (Rev. 21:27).

And then they charged me with having written this: 'In his article entitled "Faithful to death" M I Khorev writes the following, "It is better to die than to cease from worshipping the living God". '

My beloved children, don't harden your hearts when you hear these things about the persecutors of the church of Christ and their unjust dealings with Christians. Do not harden your hearts when you see Christians portrayed in the press, on radio or on television as uneducated and primitive boors who have no concern about progress and development, and when they are pictured in the worst possible light. Don't harden your hearts either when they are deprived of the right of reply and are not allowed to counter this twisted information by presenting the truth, or to challenge these lies in public debate. When you see and hear all this, and I'm sure that you have already seen and heard a lot, do not harden your hearts and do not repay evil for evil or abuse for abuse, but rather bless those who curse you and pray for those who despitefully use you. This is what the Lord Jesus Christ taught us to do.

May the Lord help you. My concern for you is that you do not harden your hearts when at a young age you are beginning to experience more and more the unjust treatment of unbelievers in your own lives. May the Lord help you keep your heart pure and receive everything in an attitude of love.

Sixteenth Letter

Beloved children, I'd like to tell you something about those transit prisons I passed through. It is no exaggeration to say that the most difficult time for any prisoner is when he is transported from one prison to another. It can be extremely cold in these transit prisons, especially in winter, and in the summer extremely hot. Both the extreme cold and the extreme heat are hard to take.

The route took me through Kishinev, Odessa, Kharkov and Rostov-on-Don. I spent a whole month in various prisons along the way and then two months in a transport camp in the Rostov area. Then I was transported further from Rostov through Volgograd and Sverdlovsk to Omsk. How long I will stay in Omsk, I don't know. God alone knows.

Let me tell about the first stage of this journey. Once convicted, prisoners really look forward to the journey. This was the case for me, too, because the atmosphere of the cells in which you are kept while your trial is being prepared is very unsalutary and debilitating. I just longed for fresh air and for camp life. But where would this camp be? In Soroky? I spent three years there. Usually prisoners have to serve time where they have committed their crimes. Though this was normally the case, it wasn't for me. The officials working in the State Prosecutor's office threatened to have me sent to the far north. Since I knew that God overrules everything for me I was ready to go straight to heaven if that was what he wanted, and by any route he chose.

Finally, on 17th May 1980, I was awakened in the middle of the night and told to get my possessions together. Everyone in the cell knew that that day transports were going to Tiraspol and to Odessa where there were strict regime camps. If Odessa were to be my destination, then it would mean a long journey ahead of me. I'd already packed my stuff. After prayer I said farewell to my cell mates (there had been six of us in the cell).

One of these inmates had drawn very close to God. His mother was a believer. As a child he had not been allowed to go to church. 'Young man, when you get older you too can go to church,' his mother had said, 'so don't go now, otherwise they will close the meeting because of children being present. What would we do then?' So time went by. He grew up without God and married a non-Christian wife. It turned out, so he said, that she was a hard-hearted woman and the cause of his two terms in prison. He was simply overjoyed to discover that I was a Christian. And he warmed to me in a special way when he found out that my only reason for being in prison was that I had stood out for our right of sending our children and young people to prayer meetings so that they too might be saved. We had frequent talks and he expressly asked me to pray for him. Our parting was very emotional. We hugged one another as if we were brothers in the faith and we both found that parting very difficult. The cell door had opened already and the guard told me to hurry, but this prisoner just would not let me go.

How mysterious are the ways of the Lord. One wouldn't dream of finding such pearls in the midst of a filthy, perverse and drunken society. These people had become playthings of vices one dare not even mention. I talked with many of them, who did not know God's way because in their whole lives they had never heard of God. And with what concentration they listened when spoken to about the Lord, even though they themselves might never receive him into their hearts. And how many of them envied me for my faith and hope.

We were brought in the dead of the night to the train going from Ivano-Frankovsk to Odessa. The prison vehicles drove right on to the platform. When I got out of the 'raven' I instinctively looked around, but didn't see any of you because you knew nothing about my impending departure. If you had known, I'm sure you would have come to see me off on this long journey.

There were about fifteen men in our compartment— too many, especially when all of them were smoking. The train left and I prayed in my heart, 'O Lord, bless this journey.' I didn't know where we were going. Most of the men had to get out in Tiraspol and only three of us were left in the compartment. That meant the journey before me was to be a long one. 'Thy will be done on earth as it is in heaven,' I sighed to God from the depths of my heart.

As morning broke we arrived in Odessa. At approximately midday a prison vehicle came to take us to the prison. It took until evening for all of these new prisoners to be processed. First of all we were all put into a large cell. And then they looked through our dossiers and we

were put into groups according to the severity of our
penalty. Then we were searched very carefully and taken
for showers. Finally at eight o'clock in the evening we
were brought into our cells, tired and hungry but content. There we had to wait a few days for further transport. As I was being searched, I asked if I could look at
my dossier to try to ascertain where I was being sent.
'Keep your nose out of it,' snorted the guard coarsely.
The prisoner standing behind in the queue pointed to me
and said, 'This man is a holy man so don't refuse his
request.' The guard wanted to know the articles by
which I had been sentenced. We spoke with one another
for a whole hour, for which I was really thankful. But I'll
tell you more about that in my next letter.

The Lord bless you in all things.

Seventeenth Letter

Beloved children, I told you about the beginning of my
journey through the various transit camps. On the
evening of 17th May I was put in a prison cell in Odessa.
It was a very large cell, filled mainly with people from
Odessa who had already been tried and were waiting for
their sentence to begin.

There was one free bunk and, after thanking God for
the journey I had just made, I slept peacefully. In my
last letter I told you about the prison sergeant whose
attitude and conduct towards me changed when he discovered that I was a Christian. He told me that my
destination was to be Rostov-on-Don. He was quite

proud of the fact that he knew several Christians from Odessa who had also been in this prison. 'Those people were real Christians! They would have even given their lives for their God!' he said.

'Who particularly are you thinking of?' I asked. And by the description he gave of one of these Christians I knew that it was Nikolai Pavlovich Shevchenko. When I mentioned his name he was deeply moved and shook my hand for a long time. This brother Nikolai Pavlovich, an elder in the church at Odessa-Peresyp, went home to be with the Lord more than ten years ago but the memory of him was still revered in there. It just goes to show how necessary the light of Christ is in this prison darkness.

I stayed in this prison until 24th May. What did I do during this time? Every day I found people to talk to. Some of the prisoners had friends who had been Christians. In 1968 they had been in prison with some of our Christian brothers.

I had the document containing my sentence with me. As the prisoners read it a few times I had to clarify it for them. It was a really good opportunity to bear witness. But I also had my opponents. It's always good for witnessing to have such people amongst those you are witnessing to because it livens up the discussion and raises unexpected questions.

So the time didn't go by unused. As I look back I am really happy with the time in this prison. It was filthy and with lots of lice. When you stood on the floor with slippers on, the lice would crawl all over your feet. In these transit camps lice are a part of life, and the prisoners got used to them. Whenever we were allowed to exercise for an hour (in a small courtyard outside) we all took off our underwear and killed the lice. But this was only the case in these transit prisons. In the camp where I now am there are no lice because it is easier to keep the place clean.

On 24th May I was transported further to Kharkov. The sergeant I described earlier accompanied me to the 'raven', wishing me all the best and putting something into my sack. In the train I unwrapped the little packet he'd put in. It contained dripping, garlic and homemade pastry. I was really glad about this man's kindness and thanked God because I saw that his heart had been touched by the conduct and words of brother Shevchenko.

When the present revival movement in our country began in 1961 the church in Peresyp, in which Shevchenko was an elder, was one of the first in Odessa to join the revival movement. Whenever I visited Nikolai Pavlovich's house I was always well received and encouraged in my work. I saw how Nikolai Pavlovich spent nights praying for the work of God.

But now my journey was continuing and I was about to make new acquaintances. I can say with full certainty that there is no such thing as 'chance' in life. In a wonderful way God has prepared the way that we should go.

So I arrived at the prison in Kharkov. It was very good that there was a shower room here. My personal effects were put through the 'roaster'.[10] Under prison conditions it is very important that this is done. When we (approximately fifty men in all) were brought into the changing-room of the shower we were told that there wouldn't be any more water for two hours.

One of the prisoners who had travelled with me from Kishinev (a real go-getter type who could never sit still for long and was always looking for new things to do) said, 'Why just waste this time? We've got a holy man and a priest in our midst. Come on, let's hear what he's got to say.' Everyone turned to listen to me, one man in particular. We had a good discussion, with approximately twenty-five listening at first but then, as interest waned, only one man was left. This man was really interested in knowing the truth.

And this is how it is everywhere I go. The Lord always gives us the opportunity of bearing witness to his love.

I stayed in Kharkov for five days in a very large cell. My travelling companion from Kishinev introduced me once more as a 'holy man', 'the high priest of God in our country', and said that if anyone wanted to know anything about the salvation of souls then they should come to me. Once more my sentence was read aloud by the prisoners and once more there was discussion and conversation . . .

On 29th May I was transported further still and was glad that this was to be the last stage of my journey to Rostov. The transit prison in Rostov was the worst of all but I'll tell you more about that another time.

'The boundary lines have fallen for me in pleasant places; surely I have a delightful inheritance' (Ps. 16:6).

The Lord be with you.

Eighteenth Letter

Beloved children, I have been writing these letters to you now for approximately two years. I wanted you to know something about the path the Lord has led me. I realise that some of the letters I've sent in the past two years haven't arrived. You've asked me to fill in the gaps. That's difficult to do but I will try.

It's two years now since I left the camp at Rostov. When I look back I can say that the Lord in his wisdom has led me. He granted me two and a half months of rest before a long and difficult journey ensued. But God gives power to the weak and to the one having no strength he grants sufficient grace.

In prison I am both happy and sad. I am happy to have been counted worthy of being persecuted and humiliated for the sake of Christ. I am sad that there is so much work to be done in the church but that there are so few workers. Oh, how I want to be a labourer in that vineyard of Christ, but more than that I want the will of God. 'Not my will, but thy will be done.'

They also put us Christians together with criminals, meaning by that murderers, rapists, thieves, embezzlers and the like. Whenever you come into a new cell you are asked the following question: 'What article were you sentenced under?' Should the answer be, 'under article 142', most of them would just shrug their shoulders and be none the wiser. Then I would go on to explain what this meant and as soon as they heard that I was a Christian and was in prison for serving God they would be amazed.

'Well, why are you here and not in a political prison?'

'Because I'm not a political activist. I'm a Christian servant in the church. We don't meddle in the politics of the state,' I would usually answer. Then the following objection would usually be raised.

'You can't separate atheism from the Soviet State. You should have the same sort of beliefs we have. Depending on how we feel, we believe we can either light a candle in church or rob a church. They don't put you in prison for these sort of beliefs! But if you try to stop atheism in its triumphal procession across the whole of the globe, then you'll be destroyed, because you are hindering the politics of our state. Its goal is to establish Communism, and Communism and religion are irreconcilable. So conditions must be created which will pave the way for religion to die out, and this is happening because churches, prayer houses and mosques are being closed, and palaces of culture, stadia, sports facilities, dance-halls are being erected in their place. Furthermore, the state lays on all sorts of entertainment—excursions, skiing holidays in the winter, mushroom-hunting holidays in the summer, celebrations for seeing in the "white nights" and celebrations for seeing out the "Russian winter"—all to help religion die out. But to look at your sentence, it seems that you have been laying on your own entertainment and services in woods and in the open air and this is against the Soviet law. What you're doing is not helping religion die out. So you're on a war-footing with atheism and with the ideological military machine of our state. This means that you Christians are directly challenging atheism, the politics of the Communist Party and the government, and by your actions you are preventing the construction of an atheistic society. This is why you are political offenders and not criminals. Therefore why they have put you into the same prison as us I don't understand . . . '

I regularly heard such arguments. In prison you meet many interesting people that you can discuss with, but usually this circle of interested folk diminishes with time as each one pursues his own interests. Then you're left with a few individuals who are more deeply interested in the faith. A few of them are very warm to the truth and are open to the message of Christ as their Saviour. They appreciate the good news of the love of God who through the blood of Christ forgives all our sins. They are amazed at how simple the forgiveness of sins is. I've prayed with some of them who told me, 'How good it is that there are those of you preaching the message of Christ amongst us criminals!'

Yes, it is no accident that God has put us together with criminals. I constantly thank God for the wisdom of his leading.

May the Lord be with you.

Nineteenth Letter

I send you my greetings, my beloved children.

In each of my letters I lovingly seek to tell you about the wonderful deeds of God. Not everything that God does is immediately comprehensible to us, but at the end of our lives every Christian will certainly cry out to the Lord, 'How great you are, O God, your wisdom is in all your ways and all your works!'

Yes, one day we will look back and see everything clearly. But how about now? Do we thank the Lord for everything now? I ask this because if we have committed our lives to him, then he never makes a mistake and he never lays a cross upon us that is too hard to bear. Never!

Now, I'd like to go back a bit to the beginning of my life. In earlier letters and talks I've already told you something about my father. His life was relatively short but it was a triumph of faith. He died in 1939 in prison in Tavda, which is in the Sverdlovsk region. He was poor and he left us no inheritance after his death. But despite that we are richer today than the richest people on earth because we know and serve the true and living God, the same God our father served.

When a child comes into the world it's a joyful occasion for the parents. And so the day I was born was no exception to this. (I am now telling you some memories that my mother shared with me.) You know that I had very poor sight from birth. The doctors told my mother, 'Your son has bad eyes but we won't be able to determine how bad or whether he can see at all until he's a bit older.' I don't need to tell you how worried my mother was. Her two daughters were quite healthy but now a son had been born who was physically 'weak'. As far as mother was concerned I was born blind.

She shared her fears with father. She often spoke of that day, saying, 'As soon as we arrived home, daddy took you in his arms and said, "Let us give glory to God for his gift to our family". '

Mother remonstrated, 'It's not only a joyful event but it's also a deeply worrying event because the boy is not healthy. They think he might even be totally blind . . . '

'Dearest, but surely you agree that God never makes a mistake?'

'Of course, God never makes a mistake but . . . '

Daddy then countered her objection and continued, 'Yes it's true our son is not as healthy as other children but his complaint is quite exceptional, isn't it?'

'Yes, but . . . '

Daddy continued, not allowing her to contradict him, 'If God doesn't permit a hair to fall from our heads without his will, then today's events are firmly in his control and I believe that our Lord has exceptional plans for our son. And now, let us give God the glory for these special plans he has for him.'

'I can't remember any longer,' mother continued, 'what passage of Scripture your daddy read but we knelt down, with you in our arms, and we thanked God for his wonderful ways in our life. I didn't share your father's joy and secretly scorned what he said. I didn't voice my feelings aloud but secretly I thought that what he said was too simplistic.'

'Now thirty years have passed and your father has long since been gone. But only now do I agree with what he said. And I feel convicted that it has taken me so long to understand why you were born with such poor eyesight and such a weak disposition. I only wish I could tell your father, "Yes, you were right with your simple faith in God. Forgive me for not understanding you, and even criticising you in my heart . . . " '

The first time my mother told me this was on New Year's Eve 1969. Naturally I rejoiced together with my mother and praised God in prayer.

Beloved children, I am telling you all this to comfort us both in the long separation we are enduring. What else can I tell you about my state of health? I have always had strength enough for my work in the churches. No one who knows me could guess how little I've been able to do in the home. My eyes have always been a great problem to me. I beg of you, beloved, take my place at home as far as you can. In a month's time I will be fifty years old. Perhaps that's why I've picked this theme for this letter . . .

The Lord be with you, beloved.

Twentieth Letter

Dearly beloved children, you've asked me to tell you something about my most difficult time in prison. I'm glad you asked me this because it's made me look back and think about, weigh and evaluate the past . . .

There are many aspects to life in the camps. Each new day brings with it new testings and new difficulties. The very circumstances in which one lives are burdensome. I'm sure you'll appreciate this when you realise that continually, day and night, I am surrounded by the criminal world. Here and there I meet an individual who hasn't been totally perverted and who also finds these circumstances difficult to live in. But such people are rare. Most of the people around me are inveterate criminals and spend most of their life in prison except for the odd interval here and there.

However, these external circumstances don't really bother me too much. I have made some really good friends amongst these criminals, discussing with them and sharing our bread rations together. Some of them even like to hear the word of truth.

Out of the various administrative departments there is one, a very large one, called the 'operations department'. Many prisoners work for this department and act as secret informers. I don't intend to go into this matter here but I'm only mentioning it so that you can get a greater insight into my life. I don't find it a great problem being watched all the while. Perhaps that's because I have got used to it since youth. Perhaps you can remember how closely I was watched during those two years prior to my arrest. Even you children noticed it.

But I would like to tell you about one incident. One day a certain Captain Vlasov, who was the deputy head of the operations department, the section responsible for the discipline amongst prisoners, said, 'Khorev, I've just received a phone call from America enquiring about you. Please inform your friends over there that this must not happen again. It was very good that I didn't clap eyes on you immediately, otherwise you would be in solitary confinement.' He was drinking as he said this and it was one month after the telephone call had taken place. I didn't bother to ask him what I would have done wrong to have deserved being put into solitary. I knew that they could bring any trumped-up reasons they wanted to justify any punishment. I think I've already told you how Vlasov cancelled one of my personal visits not so long ago because I was wearing felt boots—in winter!

But neither am I particularly bothered by not having any rights or by the lack of real nourishing food. Ha, the food! Sometimes, quite frankly, it is simply inedible. But we still eat it. Nor am I particularly bothered about the lack of vitamin content or by the total absence of fruit and vegetables. Whenever I receive a food parcel from you it's an overwhelming joy to share it with the unfortunate people around me, most of whom have been forsaken by everyone, and for whom no one cares. Quite simply, I seek to be content in all things.

I find your letters a great consolation. Sometimes, but by no means always, I receive letters sent by my brothers and sisters in the faith. Recently I received a parcel from Austria. My name was called out over the tannoy system and I was summoned to the office. There I was told that I needed Vlasov's personal permission to receive that parcel. Vlasov again! The attention and concern shown by friends abroad for prisoners of Christ in the Soviet Union is really valued and precious to me.

But there is one thing which oppresses me and gives me no rest day or night. Whenever I cross over the prison threshold and get on my bunk it means that I am cut off from my work in the church. That is the most difficult thing for me to bear. I will never get used to this. It's now twenty years since I consecrated myself fully and unreservedly to the service of God in his holy church.

In February 1962 I quit my job. I was earning a good salary and had fourteen years of unbroken service behind me. I also had a lovely wife (we had only been married for half a year). Then I gave up my prospects to enter into the ministry.

My favourite portion of Scripture are the words found in Luke 18:28, 'We have left everything to follow you.'

At first I encountered great difficulties in my new ministry since I was inexperienced, even though I had done a lot of work amongst young people in Leningrad. But the work of ministry throughout the whole vast expanse of the Soviet Union is an incomparably more difficult task. However, the Lord met me and gave me grace. The first year I worked together with brother Alexander Afanassievich Shalashov. He was a venerable old gentleman and a faithful worker in God's kingdom. He had a wealth of spiritual experience at his disposal. In 1963 he went home to be with the Lord. He used to say over and over again how few there were who forsook all to serve the Lord. Some wanted to wait until their children were grown up so that they could help them get established and get a good education. 'After that I will be free to serve God,' they say. Others promise to serve the Lord when they have retired. Others again cannot get free from their business and making money. Then there are those whose families just won't let them work any-way.

My right of residence in Leningrad was withdrawn and with it went my right of ever living again in my home city. But I'm ready to forsake all for the Lord and for his service if it benefits the church. I served four years in the Christian underground. Up to that point my life had been fairly peaceful and I could have remained with my family. But as soon as I heard the call of Christ, 'Follow me,' I got up and followed him.

The task I had was a responsible and a greatly blessed one, even though it was difficult.

Then, on 19th May 1966, I found myself in prison for the first time. However, there was still a lot of work left to do outside. The problem facing the church is still the same as at the time of Christ: 'The harvest is plentiful but the labourers are few. Ask the Lord of the harvest, therefore, to send out workers into his harvest field.' There is no way that you ever get used to the loss of your liberty. You desperately want to be free, not just to be free to do your own thing but to dedicate all your strength to the church.

Well, I think I have answered your question as to the most difficult thing for me to bear in prison.

Twenty-first Letter

Beloved children, today I want to tell you about a very important incident which was pivotal in my whole life and direction. I have already told you in earlier letters how I was set aside for the work as an evangelist on 14th July 1962.

The 14th July 1982 is a very special day for me, namely the anniversary of twenty years' service for the church of Christ. I talk about a special day, one of celebration, even though life was not at all easy. In fact it was very hard indeed. Nevertheless, when I think back over my life, I can say, 'My God is great!' I have served Jesus and he has given me strength to bear everything. And when I stand before his throne, I will say, 'My Lord! Everything that you gave me has been invested in your service . . . '

First of all, let me point out that the years 1961 to 1962 were special years for the life of our fellowship. These years marked the beginning of a revival in the church of Christ. We distributed circulars, letters and greetings, in which the initiativniki[12] attempted to encourage true Christians, and point out the unfaithfulness of the leaders of the Baptist Union of Evangelical Christians. They also admonished Christians to remain true to God and bring up their children and young people in the fear and love of the Lord. Many people read these circulars which often met with a very mixed response.

Some people said, 'What they have said is true in principle, but not possible in practice. The KGB will never allow our independence. Nice ideals, but no more than that!'

Others expressed mistrust. 'Who wrote these letters? Young people! They have some spiritual insight and they are certainly zealous, but how much experience do they have? If older responsible brothers were leading this revival movement, well then . . . '

A third group was steered secretly from the outside, and they spread the rumours amongst God's people that the signatories to these circulars were false brethren planted by the KGB to enable the authorities to discover the most active members of the church and get rid of them.

So there were a lot of people at that time who wanted to meet those behind this holy work of God to discuss all manner of questions with them. There were certainly questions, doubts and misunderstandings enough. I remember the following incident. A preachers' conference was arranged in the Baltic area. Our brother Gennadi Konstantinovich Kryuchkov was at this conference. We were sitting next to one another at the table. When I introduced Gennadi Konstantinovich to the gathering, they were all amazed. They had all expected to see an old man speak, but they heard a young one instead. By the end of that conference the next morning (it had begun the evening before), everyone was really glad that God had chosen these young men for this work.

Many Christians were very impressed at the courage of the leading brothers of the initiativniki, especially to see their willingness to leave family and job and lead the work underground, which meant being continually followed.

In the thirty years of persecution before this, believers had not been used to a life of such commitment. Many said, and still say today, 'It's better to carry on your trade and business for as long as possible because God can use you in your time off . . . ' Why do people think this way? Because they have not surrendered themselves fully to God. Without Christians who have been released from this whole economic system and are available to be sent to any corner of our great country, it would be impossible to develop a well-structured and independent ministry to the church.

I have laboured now for twenty years among the persecuted churches of our fellowship, yet these twenty years are nowhere recorded in my work register. As far as the world is concerned I have been leading an 'antisocial life', and yet these years consecrated to the service of God's people have been some of the best of my life. This is my offering to God and to the church.

I can remember one brother whom I encouraged to quit his job and dedicate himself to God's service, protest, 'But what about my family? I've got five children, a wife and an old mother to support. Someone's got to look after them . . . '

'If you will surrender yourself to the service of the church, the church will look after your family,' I said, seeking to reassure him.

'No way, church fare is really meagre. I won't subject my family to that. I don't want my wife to suffer reproach, or my children to have difficulties. They'll be asked in school where their father works and how much he earns. What would they answer? No, my hands are calloused through hard work and I . . . '

I won't tell you how our discussion proceeded. I was of a very heavy heart as I left him. All of those serving the persecuted churches also have families, wives and children, and do you think they love them any the less? They also could do the same as he and take care of their families without being separated from them, but they love the Lord more than anything else and are ready to suffer loss for the sake of Christ.

My children also have a hard time in school. How often they have to ask for time off so they could visit me. And now I am in prison again, and in comparison to me that brother is having a rather easy life. After our conversation I said to myself, 'I will carry on in the future as I have carried on in the past. It might be difficult for my children at times, and my loved ones might have reproaches hurled at them sometimes, but nevertheless I love you, Lord, more than anything else, and that is why I have left family to consecrate myself to your service.'

Beloved children, let me ask you some questions.

'Are you happy that you have grown up in the family of a man who works for the kingdom of God? You know many families where the fathers are always at home. Their situation is different from ours as is their social standing. They have no slanderous articles written about them in newspapers and they live a peaceful life.'

'Do you find the frequent partings from me distressing? I know that you love me very much, beloved, and you miss me much.'

'Would you like your life to be similar to mine?'

'So this is now my twentieth anniversary, a time of celebration for me! But let me ask you a question, beloved, may I also set the 14th July, on your behalf, as a special time of family celebration?'

I will close now and next time I'd like to tell you about some of the difficulties I have encountered in the past twenty years.

The Lord be with you.

Twenty-second Letter

Beloved children, let me continue with the subject of sacrificial living for the Lord. As a basis for my reflections I'll take the words, 'Go into the ark, you and your whole household, because I have found you righteous in my sight' (Gen. 7:1).

God decided to destroy everything that breathed upon earth, since all flesh had turned to evil in everything and the earth was full of violence (see Genesis 6:12–13). Only Noah was righteous in the eyes of God. 'I have found you righteous,' the Lord said to him. God found no other righteous people on earth, and because of Noah's righteousness God showed mercy to the whole of Noah's family. What a beautiful thought that is. I wish I were Noah so that all of my family could also be saved from the destruction to come.

During the days of Noah, life continued as normal: people ate, drank, married and gave in marriage. Houses were built, fields were ploughed. Everyone was pre-occupied with the routine things of life. But Noah, the righteous one, had other concerns. He spent several decades building a place of refuge from the impending misfortune. This he did at God's command.

He too had a family and three growing sons. Didn't he need to feed them and clothe them like other people?

Didn't he need to get them land, plant vineyards, build houses, so they could live a peaceful life and have an inheritance after his death? Had Noah preoccupied himself solely with looking after his family, his contemporaries would have praised him saying, 'What a caring father! How lucky those children are to have a dad like him!'

Well, everyone else did this, but not Noah. Instead of building three-storey villas he built a three-storey ark in which all who entered it would be saved.

Being of age, the sons could well have said to Noah, 'Father, you carry on. You've built an ark on top of a mountain and hope that some day you will be able to sail it. That's really way out! There have never been any floods on earth that have covered the mountains. Well, father, we do respect you and you carry on, but we'll stay here.'

Couldn't his children or relations have spoken to Noah like that? Of course . . . But thank God that his wife and sons and their families all decided to get into the ark of refuge. Then the day came on which God's wrath was poured out upon all living creatures on earth, and only Noah and his family were saved. How great is God's faithfulness. Through the righteousness and obedience of one man a whole family experienced grace. So Noah was wise in laying up for his family the most precious thing of all: life! So the flood passed and the earth blossomed again and Noah's sons were able to rejoice in the fruit of the earth.

Beloved children, I'd like to make this story of Noah easier for us to understand by comparing Noah's family with our own.

I was glad to do God's work and even when the time came for me to start a family I wrestled with one question: 'Would the cares of life ensnare me and keep me back from serving Christ?' I knew that anyone desiring to work in the kingdom of God could allow himself to be tied down by the everyday matters of life. So what was I to do? I saw many families where mother and father were only concerned with one another and with the children, and these families were regarded as happy ones. But I wanted a completely different way of life. I prayed about this and God heard me. Not only have family ties not tied me down (although God knows that I love my wife and children) but they have helped me in my service.

I'd like to tell you about another day in my life. It was the beginning of August 1964. I had been away from you for about two months and the usual question I was asked upon returning home was, 'How long are you home for?' This time I didn't answer definitely, but when I saw the difficult situation that my family was in I said that there was no way I could just up and leave. I had no right to do that. Neither could I neglect my service to the church. So what was I to do? We agreed to tell no one about our need but to fast and pray that God would give the solution to this insoluble problem.

I did not venture out in those days, but prayed fervently, certain that there are no dead-end streets for him nor any insoluble problems. I knew that he would certainly intervene at the right time, because that was what he had always done. After we had prayed for three days, Piskovya Alexandrovna visited us from Leningrad (later on you used to call her Babushka Pasha).

I had known her when I was a child. She often visited us in Leningrad and would babysit us four small children while our parents went to church.

We were so glad to see her again, and I asked her: 'Babushka Pasha, how long do you intend to stay? Would you like to be our guest and rest here, or have you got things to do in the area?'

'Well Misha,' she answered, 'I heard that you already had small children and so I decided to take a holiday and visit you. And if it is at all possible I would like to help you. I have got a month free.'

That was really an answer from God. That same day I returned to my ministry. From that time on Babushka Pasha became a member of our family. A month later she returned to Leningrad, resigned her job (she had been working as a home help in a fairly well-to-do household) and came straight back. Many people who saw Babushka Pasha cooking for us thought we must really be paying her well, but financially we weren't able to do this. Anyway, there was no way that all the money in the world would have paid for and employed such a person.

Babushka Pasha would often say in her prayers, 'Lord, I thank you that you have shown me where you want me to serve you.'

Yes, this beloved 'grandmother' really lifted a weight from my heart and I didn't need to worry so much about you. She stayed with us until May 1968. Then she became seriously ill and travelled back home. At that time I was in prison and it was just before my release. I was able to visit her as she lay dying. Together we thanked God. A few days later Piskovya Alexandrovna went home to be with the Lord. Yes, God had repaid us a hundredfold on earth in the person of this good and aged lady.

So, don't be surprised, beloved children, that our family is not like many others. Now you are of age and can understand that there is sacrifice involved in serving the Lord. It means forsaking everything. But I am still concerned about you, beloved. What do you intend doing with your lives? At this crucial time for our church will you consecrate your lives fully and unreservedly to building this 'New Testament ark'? It is a most desperately needed work and one that carries great responsibility with it. I have two questions to ask you: Have you been baptised? If not, are you firmly resolved to go through the waters of baptism and join the church? Then after baptism will you be prepared to forsake all and follow Christ? I ask you to answer these questions for me, and more than that answer them for yourselves.

Many sincere people who love the Lord often only express their desire to be baptised and received into the church in the summertime (in the USSR we baptise in the open air). I believe that you should make your desire known to God's people as soon as it comes to fruition in your hearts. When a young man or woman has expressed their desire to become a member of the church, then in a real way they have already bound themselves to the living body of Christ. Then responsible brothers, together with the whole church, will make every effort to care for their souls, instruct them and ensure their spiritual growth. The most important thing is that each person should decide for himself. I know of cases where people were baptised in the winter too, but these cases are rare. I have twice baptised people in icy water. Now then, may our work not be in vain before the Lord. He is on our side. To him be praise and honour.

So here's to the glorious rapture of the church of Christ! It is my greatest desire to pray together with you.

Twenty-third Letter

My beloved and precious ones, I greet you with a full heart this glorious Sunday morning. I love this day in particular and always seek to spend it in remembrance of you. Knowing this is the day that God's people everywhere have fellowship, encourage and strengthen one another, and rejoice together (fellowship with the saints is always a great joy). I also seek to be joined with you in spirit. It might only be in spirit but it nevertheless means much to me. Even as a young person I was very concerned to lead a particular kind of life, one characterised by holiness and one that did not violate the Word of God. If I wasn't totally convinced about a matter then I would always ask myself the question as to whether or not I would be happy seeing my children do it. This would very often help me to gain clarity on a particular issue.

I knew that if I walked in the fear of the Lord, then my children, too, might walk in that way. And this is true. If I were a bad man, and by that I mean one who is insincere, dishonest and cowardly, then my children would not only grow up to be the same, but perhaps even worse. Are there exceptions to this? Yes, there are. But I don't want to go into it here. Rather I'd like to think back to my youth and back to my own time of preparation. That time had enabled me to give you something meaningful in life. I have not devoted just twenty years to your upbringing (this is how long you have been on this earth) but forty years, that is, the whole of my conscious lifetime. Now judge for yourselves, beloved, if I don't have the right to be assured about you. 'Those who sow with tears shall reap with joy.' So I am always keen to hear about any good news from you and in it I seek for any signs indicating a change in your character for the better. When I find them I rejoice greatly.

You once asked me what was the most joyful thing I'd experienced during my time in prison.

I can answer this without any hesitation by quoting the words of the apostle John, 'I have no greater joy than this, than to hear that my children are walking in the truth' (3 Jn 4). A Christian can rejoice in the greatest affliction. Why? Not because he can necessarily see the end of his suffering, or that things are going to get easier for him, but because he can see the children of God walking in the truth.

These words have become especially meaningful to me behind these prison walls. I have had to give up everything, and month by month have not known whether my family was in good health or not.

'I am the way, the truth and the life,' Christ said. The only thing that many parents are concerned about is that their children should not materially be any worse off than others. That is a tragic mistake to make, because 'the kingdom of God does not consist of eating and drinking, but of righteousness and of peace and of joy in the Holy Spirit.' (Rom. 14:17). Have my children understood that? Have they surrendered their young hearts undividedly and once and for all to God? Do they want to follow Christ's path, the path which is full of thorns but also full of glory, the only one that leads to the kingdom of God and of Christ? Will my children be ashamed of sitting together with me in the dock because of their faithfulness to God? And in eternity will they take their place in the government of God? Such questions as these concern me greatly. I deeply desire, beloved sons, that you should understand what is at stake in a life committed to Christ.

Now months have passed by and I have learned that all of you are resolved to go through the waters of baptism and be joined to God in covenant. What a joy that is to me. It is a great honour for any young person to make a covenant with God while still young and then remain true to him his whole life long. May the Lord help you to fulfil this blessed desire you have expressed and dedicate your whole life to God.

I'd like to give you some pointers which I think are important. But I'll do that in my next letter. I can hardly wait to tell you everything that's on my heart so that I might keep you from error . . . However, now I am very tired and would like to go to the Lord . . . However, I still feel I need to tell you everything on my heart. The Lord be with you in everything.

Twenty-fourth Letter

My beloved children, today I have another opportunity of telling you my life-story. I do this so you can praise God who has blessed me and has kept me in all my ways and has always given me the strength and help I need. Even though he has allowed severe testings, I was never tested beyond what I could endure.

So on 30th May I arrived in Rostov-on-Don. I had often been in this city but this was my first taste of prison life here. Of all the transit prisons that we passed through I found this the most difficult.

As was usually the case they took their time unloading the prisoners. It is terrible to have to stay for a long time in those vehicles. It was terribly hot in the 'raven' because it was made out of metal, and was left standing a long time in the searing sun, with us inside.

I would just like to tell you something of what a journey in one of those vehicles is like. At the station they drive the 'raven' right up to one of the wagons of the train and then they begin loading. The first twelve prisoners would sit upon the benches that are lined up against three of the inside walls of the vehicle. And then another seven men would be loaded in. The last three really have to be squeezed in hard by the soldiers. The men inside would shout that there was no more room, but no one would take any notice of them. We'd put our personal effects on the floor where there was literally nowhere to put your feet. Somehow I managed to force myself into this vehicle and stand on one leg leaning with my hand against a wall so as not to topple onto those sitting down. The door was then locked. Our vehicle was the first one to be loaded. We then waited until two more were crammed with prisoners. It was unbearably hot because there was no ventilation. Then, to top it all, several men lit up. You could hardly breathe. Then, I switched to the other foot to rest my leg.

Finally, our vehicle set off. When you were packed in like this it was awful to go round corners because one arm was not enough to bear up all the weight of bodies pressing against you. I resigned myself to the fact that the whole ordeal would be over very shortly.

Soon we arrived at the prison, but had to wait a long while until the prison gates were opened. First of all, the other two vehicles were unloaded while our vehicle had to wait, again in the sun. Then our turn came. All the prisoners were dripping with sweat as if they'd been standing in rain. We stumbled out of the vehicle and stood to our feet. I was soaking and even my pockets were wet. I didn't bother to wipe the sweat from my face because it would have been pointless. But we'd survived the journey and were standing there, in the searing sun, yes, but at least in the fresh air.

I was longing for the registration procedure to take as long as possible, but the officer in charge took our files and began to call our names. My turn came and I called out my birthplace, year of birth, the article under which I had been sentenced, and the length of my sentence. Then I was put into a badly ventilated cell with a low, arched ceiling. The cell was crowded because several transports of prisoners had arrived at the same time. I didn't bother to count how many were in the cell, but in our wagon alone there had been between 70 and 75 men, and several wagonloads of men had been squashed into this cell so there must have been about 200 men. I managed to find a little space in the middle of the cell for my personal effects and I sat upon them. The higher you sat the less oxygen there was because everyone was smoking. The lower you were the easier it was to breathe.

Machorka-smoke enveloped the whole cell, but as well as this some of the prisoners had begun to brew up chifir, a strong concentrate of black tea, as soon as they got into the cell. Chifir has a sort of inebriating effect for a while and lifts people's spirits. To brew it you had to heat up half a litre of water by burning a handkerchief, a sock, a vest or a woollen blanket. Usually the material was soaked through with sweat and would only smoulder, emitting an acrid smoke. This stench had to be endured for several hours a day.

Then the doors were opened and we were sorted out into various categories. One and a half hours later my name was called out and I left the cell. After checking my details I was brought back in to the same cell. Approximately four hours later there were appreciably less people in the cell, only those sentenced to strict regime.

But you can get used to anything. Even during these dark hours I found comfort because I knew that it was for the name of Christ that I was in that situation. I knew it was not because of a crime of violence or theft I had committed but because I had preached the holy gospel. Thanks be to God that he counts us worthy to bear this great honour. God has given us the right not only to believe in Christ's name but also to suffer for his sake.

Towards evening we were taken to the shower room and then finally shown to our cells. From my knowledge of other prisons I expected that once in your cell you would be able to rest. But this was not the case. I was literally thrown into a fairly small cell with sets of two bunk beds. It was absolutely crammed full. For a moment I was taken aback. I didn't even know where to put my feet. The air was sticky and everyone was dripping with sweat. Immediately next to the door on the right-hand side was the toilet and wash basin. The upper bunks were not high, about chest height, probably because the ceilings were so low. For this reason the lower bunks were almost on the floor. Everywhere half naked men were lying around. Ten of us from the last transport were brought into this cell. We were simply left standing in the middle of the cell and didn't know where to put our bundle of personal effects. Then the usual introductions began: 'Who are you; where are you from; why are you here; what article were you sentenced under?' Again, everyone's attention was drawn to me, and again there were some who said they had been in prison with other Christian brothers. The name of brother Peters was the one most frequently mentioned because he had been in this prison."

I hadn't slept the night before and the whole of that day I had been tense and uptight. So I wanted to rest as soon as a place came free in one of the lower bunks. Since prisoners don't get anything to eat the day they arrive you can just imagine how exhausted I was. But God gives sufficient strength to those who are weak and weary.

The next day I had some very good conversations in that cell and in the evening I went to bed as soon as I could and fell into a deep sleep. I woke up in the middle of the night and felt somewhat strengthened. I got up straight away because someone had vacated his place for me and he himself had not been able to sleep. I had already slept six hours straight through. May the Lord be praised for this kindness to me. Yes, people you meet in prison are often rough and ready but even through them God sends his comfort. This is possible only because God's people pray for us prisoners. Thank God for the church of Christ which does not forget her prisoners.

May the Lord be with you beloved. I will try to carry on in a later letter.

Twenty-fifth Letter

Beloved children, in my last letter I told you how I arrived in Rostov prison. It really makes you feel good when you know that other true brothers and servants of God have been there before you. Through their good example and preaching about Christ they have prepared the way for later prisoners of Christ. I spent nine days in that cell in Rostov prison. I will briefly outline my experiences to you.

The light in the cell burned incessantly around the clock. At night it didn't bother me because I slept below and the upper bunks shaded me. But there were not many who wanted to sleep down below because of the bed bugs. Everyone thought there are more bed bugs down below than up above. That might be true sometimes. When there's bright light above, the bed bugs tend to hide themselves. Down below, in the shade, they can have a regular 'heyday' and many prisoners jump up out of bed because they cannot sleep.

They didn't bother me much. That doesn't mean to say that they gave me a wide berth, of course they didn't. But I didn't feel their bites. As soon as I lay down I immediately fell asleep. I was so exhausted and slept so deeply that no amount of bed bugs could have woken me up. As soon as I woke up I vacated my bed so another could sleep there. There were several waiting their turn. It was only when I got up that I saw that my whole body and all my clothes were covered in blood. You could tell what a stormy night it had been. Yet I have always been thankful to God for that particularly good night's sleep. I saw in it a special grace of God.

In that cell someone read my sentence aloud and then I had some very good opportunities for sharing. From time to time one of the guards would open the food trap (the little window in the door through which food was passed). Every day you were allowed half an hour to exercise outside. I always chose to go. During the exercise time the loudspeakers were turned on and music blared out so loudly that the prisoners, exercising in small segregated courtyards, could not shout to one another. The din didn't bother me since I was at peace.

I usually spent my time talking to one person only, but sometimes I did talk to whole groups too.

I think I mentioned that people were smoking and brewing chifir all the while in the cell. This is typical of all prisons. They play cards around the clock, and every-thing is gambled away, one's money, one's personal belongings, one's honour, and one's conscience . . .

There was no way you could stand at the wash basin in your slippers. At first I couldn't make out what all the muck on the floor around the wash basin was. It looked like it was a two-inch layer of wet dirt. Then I noticed that it was the water-sodden ashes of the cloth and paper that had been used to brew up the chifir. To get to the wash basin and use the toilet the prisoners had turned over five or six food bowls and used them as stepping stones. You can get used to anything and maintain your serenity in any situation. This was the first prison I'd been in where I saw the guards carrying truncheons and wooden hammers. And not only did I get to see these weapons, but for the first time I also experienced the crack of a hammer on my own body. I'm sure you are asking why and what regulations I had violated.

On 4th June we were taken into the showers. I didn't have any soap left, even though you had sent me ample. I had shared it out piece by piece until it had all gone because none of the others ever received any.

In the showers everyone was given a small piece of soap and we began to take a hasty shower. The water was only turned on for ten minutes. If anyone hadn't rinsed himself properly at the end of that time he had to put his clothes on over a layer of soap.

Five to six minutes had passed and some were already getting out of the shower. I gathered up some of the remains of the soap that had been thrown away and quickly washed my underwear. Then the water was turned off but I had managed to wash everything. I then began to get dressed but in the changing-room the air was so bad that I started to have heart murmurs. I got dressed but very slowly. Usually the prisoners are not taken back to the cells until everyone is out of the showers. But when I got out no one was in the courtyard and so I ran to catch them up. All the workers standing around the courtyard smiled to one another, 'Ha, he'll get the hammer.'

When I reached the basement where our cell was, a sergeant with a hammer was standing by the door. I can't tell you what he said since his words don't bear repeating! But I was beaten with the hammer while the guards all stood around laughing. I felt this blow for a long time afterwards.

The prisoners in these transit prisons have no idea as to when they will be transported on. But finally, on 8th June, I was summoned and I soon understood that there was only going to be one transport that day to the labour camp in Rostov. I was happy about that. Those of us due for transport were left that whole night in our cell and early the next morning were taken in a 'raven' to our final destination.

So I had reached the end of a very difficult and long journey. I was glad, but did not know that within two or three months I would be on another journey which was not to be any easier.

But beloved, we are pilgrims and wanderers here on earth. Our pathway goes through suffering, separation, distress and deprivation, but our goal is glorious—the kingdom of Heaven. And the wearier we become upon this pathway, the more precious, pleasant and beloved will be that place of rest. Christ will wipe away all tears from our eyes. Whoever has not wept will not have any tears to wipe away. So let us exert ourselves for the name of God. Let us reach the end of our strength so that we can present the fruit of our labour to the glory of God. God will give us all the strength we need, and with his help we will reach the end of the road victoriously. To him be the honour and the praise.

In my next letter I will try to tell you about what happened when I arrived at the labour camp in the Rostov.

Twenty-sixth Letter

I began this letter a long while ago, and today I will continue it.

What is it like in a strict regime labour camp? They differ, both in their size and in their discipline. Each camp has its own peculiarities.

The thing I liked best of all in the Rostov camp was the large exercise area. There was even a little place to sit which was, of course, a rarity in strict regime camps. Perhaps you have noticed that I have never described prison food to you or said whether there was enough of it. I did this quite deliberately because we are not to become slaves of our stomach. The apostle Paul wrote that he had learned to be content in all things, whether in plenty or hunger, whether in abundance or want, 'I can do everything through Christ who strengthens me' (Phil 4:13). It is really important for us to imitate Paul and be content in any circumstances we might find ourselves in. 'The kingdom of God does not consist of eating and drinking but of righteousness, peace and joy in the Holy Spirit' (Rom 14:17). That means that if you go hungry and do not have enough to eat day after day this should not affect your spiritual state negatively.

I would often go to bed on an empty stomach. I can sleep even if I have hunger pangs. When I woke up it could well be that I was happy not to go to breakfast because I no longer felt hungry. When we reached the Rostov labour camp we were kept in quarantine for seven days. The cell reserved for new arrivals (there were fifteen of us) was in the same building as the solitary confinement block. This building had a long corridor with doors which bolted on both sides. It was just like a prison in a prison. We were not allowed to take our bags of personal effects into the cell but had to leave them in a corner of the guard room. Two hours later the cell door was opened and we were allowed to collect our belongings. They had been searched and everything the guards might need for their own personal use had been confiscated. This was a minor detail, but I mention it to give you an idea of what life was like in these camps.

Every morning I would get up at about five o'clock, before everyone else, to pray and get some fresh air. It is especially beautiful to have fellowship with God early in the morning. I needed to be alone. It was the middle of June with beautiful weather and clean air, which was something I had really missed. So I could take very long walks and that gave me enormous pleasure. It seemed as if I just could not get enough fresh air. I wanted to breathe and breathe as deeply as possible. Many people who have been exhausted through these long transport journeys also do the same.

I also had good talks in the camp. Prudence dictates that I do not mention the names of the people, but I always remember them in my prayers. One prisoner said, 'How fortunate I am to have heard the truth about forgiveness of sins put in such a simple way. I am not at all sorry that I came to prison because I have come to know here what I could never have learned outside. The only places I would frequent outside were clubs, palaces of culture, sports stadia, beer halls, restaurants, parks and open-air swimming pools and the like. The only time I heard about God was in a dirty joke.'

One very tall young man comes particularly to mind at this time. One evening when it was already getting dark he came to sound me out on my convictions. He asked why our churches didn't get registered and why we were tried. Finally, he admitted that he had been a police collaborator and had broken up young people's meetings as well as dragging them off to police stations. He explained that he had never really understood why these young people were being persecuted. His superiors simply told him that Christians were American agent provocateurs and spies. But when he discovered that the young people were later released, he began to have second thoughts and suspected that perhaps his superiors were hiding something and even deceiving him. We had to part and he asked my forgiveness that he had allowed himself to be so fooled. He was quite surprised that I maintained a friendly attitude towards him.

I can also remember a murderer that I met. He had received a very stiff sentence. I don't particularly want to cite all the details of his crime. He himself knew full well that he had done a terrible thing. We often met and he would tell me a lot about himself. Once when we met I asked him to listen to me and not interrupt until I had finished. So, as best I could, I told him about the love of God, the fall of man, the penalty for sin, the shed blood of Jesus Christ and the Book of Life in which the names of all the saved are written. We ended up talking the whole evening and only separated once curfew sounded.

At five o'clock in the morning I went for my usual walk, and saw him. He hadn't slept the whole night. He just could not understand how sins could be forgiven so simply. 'If God demanded great sacrifices of us for the forgiveness of our sins, I could understand it,' he said. 'But it's all so simple. All we have to do is admit our guilt and then the blood of Jesus Christ washes away all our sin . . . '

I told him about God's plan and that 'it pleased God, through the foolishness of preaching, to bless those who believe' (1 Cor 1:21). Then a long conversation ensued. I think this particular man found forgiveness of sins in Christ.

Beloved children, I wonder if you could write and tell me what you make of this part of Holy Scripture: 'the foolishness of preaching'. Why does God have such a plan of salvation? Could you really think about this and let me know in full your answer? I'll wait for your reply.

Beloved children, I have told you my dealings with prisoners. But I also had long conversations with camp leaders. I'll tell you about this next time. The Lord keep you.

Twenty-seventh Letter

Dear children, I send you many greetings and am continuing this letter which I began a long while ago. When will I reach the end of my story? I don't know. Probably only when I am released and see you again. But in the meantime . . . May the Lord help us not only to enjoy receiving letters from one another but also enable us to maintain a heart, goal and purpose in life for him.

In my last letter I told you something about my relationships with prisoners. I have pleasant memories of the camp in Rostov. In one way you can say that the Lord gave me two and a half months' holiday before I set out on another long journey.

In this letter I'd like to tell you about some of the contact I had with people in the administration.

One time I was allowed into the operations department. There the officer questioned me about my family and private life.

'Comrade head of department,' I said, 'I'm not deceived into thinking that I have been invited to a social club by coming here. I know this is the operations department. So would you please get on and tell me quite plainly why you have called me here?'

'To get to know you.'

'If you want to get to know me you can question my group leader. No one gets sent to the operations department for this reason.'

He smiled, 'Well, what do you think about this operations department? Do you know what functions we carry out?'

He was obviously dropping broad hints and wanted to know whether I would collaborate.

'I know full well what the functions of the operations department are,' I answered. 'But I will not collaborate with you, either now or later on. This is what the gospel which we follow with all of our hearts teaches us, and it is also our deep conviction. We don't look at sin lightly. We want to convict sinners of their sinful ways, so we will never support crime. But we Christians have a different way of reforming criminals than you do. We don't believe in informing on people. So I want to tell you quite straightly from the outset what I think.'

We parted on good terms. He intended to call me to the operations department again, but never got round to it.

Should you not know what the operations department is, I will describe it briefly. In their relationships, prisoners keep a close watch on what the others say and do. Everyone wants to know who has said and done what, who has brought this or fetched that, where this person is going to or where that person has come from, what so-and-so's plans are, and so on. The operations department then gleans all this information from its various agents and secret collaborators.

Far be it for me to condemn them for this, but that is how they operate. In the outside world that's the way the KGB works. The KGB has its informers everywhere, even in the church. But that's another matter altogether. Perhaps one day I'll tell you about that, too.

Did you notice how straight I was when speaking with this officer and how I made it very clear to him from the outset what I thought of collaboration? Was it really necessary to be so straight?

Dear sons, let me tell you that Jesus Christ withstood the Devil's temptations because he gave such a straight reply. 'It is written . . . It is written . . . It is written . . . ' On three separate occasions the Devil came to him with various temptations and three times Christ countered these attacks with the Word of God. There was nothing superfluous in their dialogue. Finally he said, 'Away from me Satan!' Their dialogue was short but the victory was great.

But if we look at Eve it is a different story. She lost against the Devil because she spoke too much, expressed her fears and came with many ifs and buts. So she was defeated. It is very important that wherever a young person goes he makes it immediately clear that he is a Christian. Then it will be a lot easier for him later on.

A young man once told me what it was like when he entered the army. In the railway truck he was too embarrassed to admit that he was a Christian. He laughed with the others at dirty jokes. His conscience condemned him, but it was even more difficult afterwards for him to tell his comrades that he was a Christian. The situation became more and more difficult with every passing day and the result was that he turned to worldly living. He never really recovered properly.

I'd like to tell you the story of a brother who used to work in our church so that you can understand how important this is. From youth he had been brought up as a Christian. At the age of thirty-six or thirty-seven he became an elder. He really loved his large church very much. When the troubles began and the threats increased, he was, to begin with, very much on his guard and he told me how God gave him wisdom to skirt around the 1929 legislation. 'These laws are really sinful,' he said, but as time went on he gradually entered into a dialogue with those responsible for religious affairs. I was amazed when he said, 'They call me to the relevant department and go on at me for the active religious work I am doing in the church, (such as evangelistic meetings, children being in the services, baptising without informing the authorities, and many other things). They tell me that these activities are punishable under article 142 of the Penal Code of the RSFSR (Russian Republic). I listen to them very carefully and then tell them that I come from the country and am doing everything as best I know how. I also tell them that I have never heard of such a clause. They for their part smile at my "stupidity" while I go on pretending to be a simpleton, but secretly laugh at them. David too once pretended to be mad. What do you think, brother? How would you behave?' he asked me.

'In such matters as these I would be quite decisive and quite direct,' I answered. 'I would tell them that I would never keep that legislation because it contradicts the teaching of Christ.' The elder didn't agree with me and thought it unwise to be so open with the enemy.

'Your enemy should not know what you are thinking nor what you intend to do.'

Sometime later we met again. He suggested that I should speak in his church, and I did. Many questions came up, such as the question of sending petitions, the question of the persecuted brethren and the whole question of one's attitude towards registration and the law.

After this church meeting the elder was summoned to the authorities and asked why the Christians in his church sent in petitions. He answered, 'I myself have never sent a petition. I believe that we must trust God more than we do, and that he will intervene. But others see things differently, and so as to maintain unity I give them permission.'

'And why do people in your church talk negatively about the 1929 legislation governing religious cults?'

'I am afraid that I don't know all the ins and outs of all of this legislation, so I cannot really comment. But if guests come and say something about this, then that is their business.'

The church in which this brother is an elder is a large church and so he suggested to them that they appoint someone to help him.

'It is too much for me because I am already old,' he said, seeking to justify his request. A helper was chosen, a man who was a very determined servant of God.

Shortly after this, the elder was summoned again to the authorities and was confronted with the same accusations. This time he laid the blame squarely on the shoulders of his helper. 'I am only concerned with theological matters. My helper deals with all the other matters because I cannot understand these legal matters.'

Shortly after this his helper was arrested and sentenced under Article 142.

When I met that elder again, and asked how things were going in his church, he remarked that he was happy and still thought that the younger brothers were unwise and didn't know how verbally to outmanoeuvre the authorities. He regarded himself as exemplary in this. 'You simply have to pretend that you are a nincompoop or crazy or something, but in your heart you know full well what you are doing . . . '

Well, that was his opinion, but the time will come when our deeds will be judged for their true worth in the righteous light of God's court, and not at all in our own light. When God judges them they might well be revealed as a betrayal of Christ and his workers in the harvest field. And if it is only then that we discover this it will be a terrible situation to be in because there will be no changing it.

Beloved children, fear every kind of impurity. Especially fear any deviation from the straight ways of God. The authorities could well see through the manoeuvrings of this particular servant of God. For a while they tolerate such people whose fearfulness allows the heads of other people to roll. Such people are no danger to the authorities. This elder is still alive today, but it is really sad to see him. He is living in continual fear and that is an awful burden to carry. It is true that Christ will not 'break the bruised reed', but it is also impossible for anyone to rely on a bruised reed. The only thing that it's good for is to be burned. Think of the words of John in our Russian Bible, 'The man who fears is not made perfect in love!' (1 Jn 4:18).

This is how I understand things. If I serve in the church of Christ then I am duty bound fearlessly to defend the people of God during difficult times. It is my duty to teach the church, and show by my example, that they should endure testings. Every church member should be exhorted to love his neighbour and to be prepared to defend his brothers and sisters by all possible means. This defence might be by a word of encouragement, or by sending petitions to the authorities which convict them of their wrong and at the same time bear witness to the love of God. A person should do this openly and fearlessly, even if it means being the first one to be brought to account. 'The hireling is not the shepherd . . . ' (Jn 10:12). ' . . . the good shepherd lays down his life for the sheep' (Jn 10:11). The good shepherd should not use the device of cunning, nor should he expose others to danger to save his own skin. He must be ready to make any sacrifice at any time in the course of his duty. My dear sons, keep your hearts and your consciences clear.

I wanted to carry on writing, but I am afraid my eyes are too tired.

Twenty-eighth Letter

Beloved children, let me carry on my reflections. A short while ago I wrote a letter to you in which I told you about the most joyful time I ever experienced in prison. As I told you, there is no greater joy for me than to hear of God's children walking in the truth.

I really was overjoyed to hear the news, my beloved sons, that you have applied for baptism and for membership to Christ's holy church. It is a special joy for every father and mother to witness the day when their children surrender their lives to God of their own free will. I am afraid my father was not able to witness that day, but God has given me this grace.

But in the midst of all my joy it is my duty to point out to you some dangers which lurk along life's way for a Christian. Take special note of what the apostle John says: 'The children of God live in the truth.' I regret to say that not all who call themselves Christians live according to the truth. I will only be really happy, finally and eternally, when you have not only been baptised and received into the church membership but also when you are walking in God's truth.

The apostle Paul was also grieved that many Christians 'sought their own pleasure and not the pleasure of Jesus Christ'. Beloved sons, don't ever let yourselves get into this tragic state of affairs.

Living according to God's truth means that my ego must die, and I must live entirely for God and for my neighbours. Living according to God's truth means not following the crowd and not being dismayed when even your friends misunderstand you. For the God whom you serve will have the final word. On the day of judgement he will speak the final word over the whole of your life.

Jesus Christ gave two appraisals of his servants: 'You good and faithful servant' and 'You evil, lazy servant.' Each one, according to the appraisal he got, received his reward or punishment. Just think of the parable of the talents. Each one of us is free to use the talents entrusted to him in his own way. The Lord will not restrict anyone.

But at the right time God will call each one of us to give account.

I really want you to be children of God that live such holy and faithful lives and work in such a way that Christ will be able to say of you on that glorious day, 'You good and faithful servant, go, enter into the joy of your Lord!' That is my prayer.

We know, both from the Bible and from our own personal experience, of many negative examples where people began in the spirit and ended in the flesh. Let me just cite a few examples to you by way of admonishment.

Elisha and Gehazi. Both these servants of God prayed to the same God. They brought their sacrifices to him at the same altar. Both were respected among the people, but the behaviour of one was in direct contrast to that of the other.

Naaman, the Syrian army commander, was healed of a serious disease called leprosy and offered Elisha great riches for his healing. Elisha refused. 'As true as the Lord lives, I will receive nothing from you.' And the fortunate Naaman travelled home, thanking God.

Riches have spoiled many in this world. They tempted Gehazi, too. He saw that Naaman was a very rich man and decided to retrieve for himself at least something of what his master had refused. He said to himself, 'As true as the Lord lives! I will run after him and accept a gift from him.' Gehazi called God to be his witness in the same way as Elisha called God to be his witness, but both of them acted in totally different ways. I don't need to tell you what happened later on. I will simply remind you that Elisha had power even after his death. (Can you remember how a man was thrown onto the grave of Elisha and came back to life as soon as he touched Elisha's bones?) But Gehazi's offspring were afflicted with leprosy to the fourth generation.

The problem with some of God's children is that as their lives progress they ever increasingly repress the presence of God in their lives. Just think of God's words, 'These things you have done and I kept silent; you thought I was altogether like you.' (Ps 50:21). A Christian who acts falsely and is not punished immediately (as Ananias and Sapphira were) is in danger of abusing God's patience and gradually drifting so far away from the truth that one eventually doubts that he ever knew the truth. The judgement of God will be, 'You evil and lazy servant.' And the resulting reward will be a very hard one to bear. If laziness were the only sin of that servant—he camouflaged his by many excuses.

Many Christians today will only do those things which bring them prestige and keep them out of difficulty. They preach sermons which cannot be faulted and they have the skill of calling people to a decision. But the most important thing lacking in their lives is a readiness for personal sacrifice. And when they are asked to sign a petition on behalf of persecuted Christians and to submit it to the authorities they have a whole host of excuses ready. One might say that there is no one really to phrase it properly without making mistakes. Another might say that it is better to wait and see and get to know the facts before writing. A third might say that it is too late to write because the brother is already in prison. There are many other excuses. And these people are just not willing to admit that they are afraid of persecution. If only they had the courage to admit the real reason for not writing: fear!

We should not be quick to judge them. But I must tell you in all seriousness that many will hear God's judgement soon: 'You evil and lazy servant!' And what will they say? Will that revelation be totally unexpected and surprising? No, there is nothing unexpected for that servant. The Lord had sought to convict him during his lifetime that there was something wrong with his Christian service, but to no avail.

Be afraid of laziness and insincerity. You will certainly be confronted some time in life with the choice between one's own personal happiness or the defence of God's truth. My prayer for you is that you should always choose to defend God's truth so the Lord will be able to say to you, 'Well done, my good and faithful servant. You have been faithful in little and I will set you over much . . .'

Twenty-ninth Letter

'Rejoice and be glad, because great is your reward in heaven . . . ' (Matt 5:12).

Beloved children, I greet you with all my heart and all love which the Lord has given to us, this precious love.

I know that you always wait eagerly for my letters and that you get quite anxious when they are delayed in coming. I'm glad that you rejoice when you receive these signs of life from me . . . It was really precious for me to hear how carefully you keep my letters and with what love you read them over and over again.

Over the years I have also received letters from you. You sent me some of your first drawings (a little house, trees, birds) when I was in prison, and also some special letters where you drew around your little hands on a piece of paper. The first words you ever wrote to me were in capital letters, the words, 'God is love.'

Now the years have gone by and I am in my third term of imprisonment for the sake of the Word of God. Now you have grown up and can think things through for yourselves and make your own decisions. I thank God. But 'small is the gate and narrow is the road that leads to life, and only a few find it' (Matt 7:14). And you, my beloved sons, thanks to the grace of God, have found this narrow, thorny way.

This is the year you have decided to get baptised. It is a pity that I cannot be there on the river bank when it happens, but I am happy that I can still tell you in letters, at least, what are some of my greatest desires for you. When you were younger you were obedient to me. I hope that you will remain obedient, even now, so please listen to what my desires are for you.

'Follow me!' These are the words that Jesus Christ spoke to his disciples. This command also applies to you. What does it mean to 'follow the Lord?' It means to share his joy and his suffering, to bear honour and dishonour for his name.

It is an honour when you are with Christ. When Christ is glorified and appears in his majesty (as a long time ago on Mount Tabor) then you will be with him and you too will be glorified. When hosannas are sung to him, as he enters into Jerusalem, you too will be there and share his honour.

But, beloved children, be prepared to stand at Christ's side when he is sentenced by Pilate, and when he is falsely accused, smitten with rods and spat upon. Stand by his side when such times come and do not be dismayed when this or that absurd charge is brought against you, or when you feel a beating on your back. Follow him and you will be blessed. Receive joyfully every opportunity you have to glorify Jesus Christ, whether it be through suffering, through deprivation or through humiliation.

Beloved children, we all look forward to Christ's return on earth and the rapture of his disciples to heaven. Then we will always be with Christ and with his saints in eternity. I would like to ask you, 'What will you have when you appear before him?'

Christ told his disciples to lay up treasure in heaven (Matt 6:20). This means that it is not here that we are to open a private account but up there in heaven. Up there in heaven all the customers' savings are guaranteed. 'Be rich towards God!' was what Christ told his disciples in Luke 12:21.

Can you remember how two angels came to Lot's house in Sodom and how the men of Sodom wanted to do them ill, asking Lot to release them to them? These men were struck with blindness while the angels carried on with their ministry which God had commissioned them to do. Angels do not have the privilege of suffering for Christ, but we do. Let us make sure that we make use of this privilege and rejoice when we have to bear suffering, blows, parting, separation and other deprivations.

I often think of Stephen, the deacon in the New Testament church. He was stoned and yet prayed for his persecutors, 'Lord, do not count this sin against them . . . ' None of Stephen's persecutors was struck with blindness, nor did any of them die through the wrath of God. Only Stephen died and it says that as he lay dying he saw heaven opened and had a vision of Christ. Stephen received his reward in heaven. Millions of Christians have followed his example by carrying the good news, with much torture, through the corridors of time to us in our generation. Each one of them has received his reward.

'What will you have when you appear before him?' I ask again. In heaven we will live forever. We will often talk with those saints about our life on earth (for we will still have the ability to remember). What will we talk about? I don't think we will discuss our house, even though that might have been a nice place to live, or our car. It won't be necessary to talk about the position we held in society, or about the riches we had. What will be a worthy theme for our conversation up there in heaven? It will be the times we were ready to sacrifice and suffer torture, the times we opened our homes for Christian meetings when all other homes remained closed, the occasions we rejoiced in the midst of tribulation.

I think that such Christians will bow before Christ and say, 'I praise you Lord, that you counted me worthy of this honour while I was on earth and that you were present with your people in my house.'

A life of sacrifice here on earth will be a matter of triumphal joy in heaven.

Unfortunately I must close here, but you can carry on this subject yourselves and develop it. I will wait until my next letter.

I close with this request: rejoice and be glad when, for Christ's sake, you suffer abuse, pain and bitterness. It might be that your name will be spoken evil of on the radio or television or in the press because of your service for God. It might be that you will be fined or demoted in your job, or even dismissed. Perhaps you will be sentenced to fifteen days or even several years of imprisonment. When this happens, rejoice in everything. It is our privilege to suffer for Christ. Take this privilege when it comes to you, my beloved sons.

I wait for an answer from you. I would love to know what you think about the matters I have raised in this letter.

Thirtieth Letter

My dear children, peace be with you. I want to tell you more about my ministry for the Lord and some of the dangers I have encountered. 'Difficulties' would be a more appropriate word than 'dangers'. No matter how capable a preacher is, he will always encounter obstacles in his service for God. And more than that, the difficulties he will encounter will grow in proportion to his capabilities.

Whenever a person begins his preaching ministry he will most certainly meet failure. He won't always be able to express what is in his heart. But that is not necessarily a bad thing. Sometimes it is good for a preacher to be in some uncertainty about his ministry. Then he will look for reasons as to why perhaps his sermon did not communicate well. Or perhaps he will dig deeper into the Word of God and prepare himself more fully. I experienced all this in my younger years. It is most important not just to preach God's Word anyhow. If your listeners fall asleep during your sermon then don't reprimand them. Perhaps they fall asleep because you did not present your subject matter in an interesting and lively way. Perhaps your sentences, though very beautifully formed, were without fire.

As the years have passed, I have sensed a greater and greater responsibility for my sermons. Our services rarely end punctually and I am usually the last to expound the Word. So I always aim at not preaching for more than thirty minutes. You have to preach in such a way that the church would happily hear more.

At the beginning of his ministry each preacher not only meets difficulties, but sometimes he may encounter great success. During some services brothers of different ages with various spiritual experience have their turn to preach, and it might be that it is one of the youngest ones whose preaching impresses the listeners most. This young man then reaches a very difficult moment as to how he will cope with this praise. Will he give himself the glory that belongs to God? Will he look down upon the other preachers?

I often remember a summer service that took place in Riga, which four of us visited. At the time we were young lads from Leningrad. All four of us were asked to preach the Word. I was to preach last and then close in prayer. It was the first occasion I had preached in front of such a large congregation. As I stood behind the very high pulpit and looked across the large hall, which was jam-packed, I was very nervous. I had preached before, but always to young people at home or to friends. But here there were more than a thousand people in front of me ... I read John 3:14: 'And just as Moses lifted the serpent in the wilderness, so must the Son of Man be lifted up.' I soon lost my inhibitions and after about two minutes was speaking with great freedom and passion. People in the hall began to weep and sob. I spoke for about twenty minutes and then closed in prayer. I knelt down to pray. And then, oh horrors, the thought came to me that I had been the best preacher that day. I wanted to banish the thought and tried to join in with the prayers that were spoken aloud, but the thought stubbornly persisted in my consciousness.

'It was only your message that really gripped the listeners,' a subtle voice whispered to me, 'just listen to those prayers ... ' I tried my hardest to drive those unworthy thoughts out of my mind, but, believe me, it just wasn't so easy.

As we left the hall, many were waiting to shake my hand and thank me for the message. One older sister said to me, with tears in her eyes, 'Dear brother, I have waited fifteen years to hear a message like that! Today through you the Lord told me what I have waited for him to say for many years.'

Beloved children, at that time I was about the same age as you. Just imagine what is is like to get praise like that. It cost me a lot of self-discipline not to take some of the glory for myself. The Lord says, 'I give my glory to none other' (Is 48:11). And woe to the person who lets his giftedness go to his head and lets others know it too. To whom much is given, much will be required.

No doubt you remember which trees will be cut down and destroyed together with their roots. It will be those which either bear no fruit, or inedible fruit. But another sort of tree will also be cut down, the one which shortly before had borne some of the most beautiful fruit. It was so fruit-laden that it simply could not bear the load and broke in two under the weight. I have seen people who have suffered inner damage because they could not bear the spiritual weight put upon them. I would venture to say that if I had attributed just one small success to myself instead of to God, that could have led to my personal downfall. A tree that bears fruit richly has its branches supported so that it can bear the whole load. I have always needed such support, and still need it today.

It's only now that I begin to appreciate my mother's wisdom and goodness. Her influence on my behaviour was unobtrusive, guiding my steps in the right direction. I wasn't aware of this and I thought I was making my own way.

For example, one time mother was reading a passage of Scripture to us (she would always read the Word of God aloud) in which Christ taught us to do good, especially to those who could not pay back. Mother asked me what I understood by this passage. I told her my answer and she agreed with my explanation. Then she said casually, 'Young man, don't you think you should behave in the same way? Just look at young people today. They usually go around with those who have a reputation or who are self-confident, not with those who are shy. Those who are a little bit more timid or unpretentious are just forgotten about. Why? It is not fair. You should try to gather those together who come from children's homes or don't have any friends, or are somewhat inhibited. They are the sort who come to services and then disappear immediately afterwards to go home. It is just incredible how lonely a young man or woman can be. There might be many reasons for this, but one of them is your own indifference . . . '

I was eighteen years old. I wanted to know how I could take up her idea. So she gave me some advice. The idea really gripped me and a week later approximately thirty young men and women gathered together in our room. I deliberately didn't address them as brothers and sisters as many of them were not yet converted but were looking for the truth of God.

It was a wonderful evening. When young people come together they usually sing a lot, but we were so engaged in discussion that we didn't even sing one song because we didn't have the time. Since that time I have had a special delight in making for those who are disregarded by everyone else.

Why am I writing this to you? Not just to dredge up my youth again. But I am concerned about you and about your life. Have you set your heart on God's large harvest fields? This is really a matter of concern to me because you are at the age and point in your ministry when what you do now will influence the rest of your life. I hope that you are reading my letters, advice and warnings with the utmost attention and seriousness.

I wanted to end this letter, but can't do so until I have mentioned one event from my early youth. When mother saw my zeal and passion for the Lord she made me a special object of her attention. One evening, when I had already gone to bed, she came to my bedside and said very lovingly and tenderly (she obviously feared that I might misunderstand her), 'Young man, please don't become a teacher. There are many reasons for this. The first and most important is that you are only eighteen years old. You are still young and it is not seemly for you to teach older men and women. Secondly, you don't have sufficient knowledge to permit you to answer every question. Then, most important of all, it is written, "Let not many of you become teachers . . . " ' I can't remember what I answered, but I was not totally happy with what she said. It seemed that she wanted to quench the spirit in me out of purely maternal feelings. In mother's eyes, I thought, I would always remain the 'baby'. But in our family it was not the done thing to contradict one's mother since she was the head of the family. Since then decades have passed and how do I now react to what she said? My mother's admonition was a great help to me in my younger years. I have often thought of what she said, especially after I was set apart to God's service. Although mother had not had a very high education she had a lot of experience in life and she lived close to God.

Sometimes a young man will be showered with questions, such as, 'How do you understand this or that passage of Scripture?' Or, 'How one should react to this or that situation?' and so on. It is a good thing when a young man has the courage to say that he doesn't know. It's right and honest to say that. But sometimes it is hard for young people to admit that they don't know, and this is when the mistakes begin. It is also dangerous, not only because you can give a person the wrong teaching or wrong advice, but also, and perhaps more importantly, because you can do yourself a lot of damage too. It might well be that in future a young man will not be alerted to danger if from his youth he has only been used to giving advice, even when he did not have the experience.

I'd like to remind you of Moses. Once some people came to him, as the leader of the people of Israel, and asked him whether they could celebrate the Passover together with the Israelites. What did Moses answer? He said, 'Wait here until I go up the mountain and consult the Lord.' His modesty was quite amazing and it was one which only characterises the spiritually strong. Moses was not afraid of the people thinking any less of him. Here was a man who had seen God himself, had decided on weighty issues, worked great miracles and also written down the Law as dictated by God. And here is this man, not knowing how to answer such a simple question!

Only very few young people are capable of such humility. Most young people are full of youthful zeal which drives them to make rash decisions.

Just to illustrate further. If my watch does not work properly it is only me who gets led astray. However, if the clock in the living-room shows the wrong time then the whole family is affected. Now, if the clock on the town clock tower is wrong then the whole city is affected. And if the wrong time is given over the radio then a whole country can be led astray.

I think you understand what I mean.

Now there is no way that I want you to become overly passive because of this letter for fear of making mistakes. Imitate Moses and don't be afraid of admitting when you don't know something. This will be highly esteemed in the eyes of God and in this way he will be able to prepare you for greater things.

Until tomorrow. In the meantime I hug you, beloved children.

Thirty-first Letter

Beloved children, I greet you with all my heart, and with the love which grows within me as you grow. As you grow in age so my concern for you and for your future also grows. I am at peace in that I know you obey us as parents and are at peace with one another, ready to help, hard working and reliable in your work. There are many good things I see in your lives, but that's not enough. Childhood is now finally behind you, and you are young men. I'd like to welcome you, beloved, into this new period of your lives. From now on you will encounter new and unknown difficulties.

The apostle John directed his teaching to believers of all ages when he said, 'I write to you, children . . . ' 'I write to you, fathers . . . ' 'I write to you, young men . . . ' To the last he said, 'I have written to you, young men, because . . . you have overcome the evil one.' In this remark he is not referring to all young men, but only to those who have overcome. Notice how the Evil One attacks them in a special way. Obviously the young men that John is referring to came away victoriously from this difficult encounter with Satan. But there were some who did not keep their youth spotless. There might have been various reasons why they fell. Some might have been overtaken by arrogance or too high a view of themselves, others perhaps succumbed to the lure of riches, while others might have given in to the lusts of youth and self-indulgent passion. How many young people have been ruined by the Devil before their lives have hardly begun. It is imperative for young people to put a bridle on their feelings, desires, lusts, passions, and inclinations. Whoever once has tasted the bitter fruit of sin or the poison of lust which brings death, will have a very difficult time for the rest of his life.

The apostle Paul admonishes Timothy, a young worker in God's kingdom, that he should not just calmly walk away from lusts which wage war against the soul, or just maintain a cease-fire when they threaten to penetrate his heart, but rather that he save himself by 'fleeing'. Why? Because young people expose themselves to great danger when they confidently believe they can keep their feelings in check by their own self-effort. Whoever depends on his own strength behaves foolishly and falls into a devilish trap. I have always taught young people to be careful and keep a check on themselves.

Sometimes young men say that they can control their desires through their reason and so they don't need to fear. They are really overly self-confident. They like to be alone with the girls and think they know how far they can allow their feelings to go, and when they need to bring them in check. But no, no, and again no. Why deceive ourselves? One must flee youthful lusts as soon as possible and not indulge in them to a 'permissible' limit. There is no way one can permit these feelings, even for a minute, to abide in one's heart. It is imperative to be on one's guard continually, and when these temptations come to reject them immediately from one's mind, not giving them a chance to gain a footing in our hearts. It's only those young men and women who keep themselves pure (by that I mean keep their hearts and thoughts pure by guarding what they look at and keeping a check on their inner feelings) who can look forward to a blessed future. It is only the fear of God that can keep you from the corruption at work in the world through lust.

From earliest youth I have always sought to walk in the fear of God and be one of that small group of victorious Christians.

I have already told you how great an influence my mother had on developing my character. Even though she was completely uneducated, she worked for us day by day, not only concerned about our health but also always concerned about our souls. She was even very concerned about what we thought.

One day I happened to be deep in thought about something. My mother noticed this and asked me what was up. I responded, 'Mother, why do you ask me what I am thinking? It can be really hard sometimes to tell someone what you are thinking. And to tell a lie would be sin. You are really putting me in a very difficult situation . . .'

'Young man, I am responsible before God for you,' she said with a sigh, 'and it is important for me that you are not only clean on the outside but also that your soul is clean. Your inner life is always open before God and you know that. So what could you be thinking about that you wouldn't want me to know about? When you have children of your own, then you will know what a serious matter it is. Do you understand that your children will be as open to you as you are to me? Now you cannot understand the depth of my concern for you, but I ask you to obey me as you have always obeyed me. And until now you have hidden nothing from me.'

At that time I was eighteen years old and really sought not to hide anything from my mother. To be quite frank I didn't always find that easy. One time I came home at midnight. Mother wasn't asleep. She knew that the evening service had long been finished and that I should have been home at about eleven o'clock. But I was late. She served me my supper, sat down with me at table and then asked, not from curiosity but as a close friend concerned about every step I made, who I had talked to and whether I had had to see anyone home. In brief, she was concerned about everything I had done . . .

How loving and caring my mother was. How many parents lose their children, thinking that they are already grown up and that they should no longer interfere in their lives, even though these children are only eighteen or twenty years old. What a huge mistake.

Admittedly, mother wasn't always the most tactful in the things she said to me, but she was always a vigilant, guardian angel. One time she said to me, 'Young man, promise me that you will never think of marrying before the age of twenty-five.' I promised her that. At that time I was twenty. I am very thankful for her warning. After I had promised her this I sought to keep it, and it wasn't until I was actually twenty-seven that I first turned to God in prayer asking him to give me a life's partner. And he gave me one for whom I thank the Lord.

Beloved children, I really desire that you be open in all things. This will keep you from many errors. You have a lot of energy, a lot of ideas and strength, but you don't have a lot of experience yet.

I have often heard young people quarrelling with their parents, 'I am eighteen years old already and you are still treating me like a small child. I know what to do. Don't ask me where I was and what I was doing. I won't tell you. Just don't ask me where I am going. I am old enough to live my own life . . . ' Do you ever have such thoughts as this? If you do, you must repent of them immediately and begin over again. You are very fortunate if you have a God-fearing mother who not only guards you from mishap in the time of your childhood, but also helps keep your heart spotless while a youth.

Thirty-Second Letter

Greetings to you my beloved.

I'd like to tell you about my mother again in this letter. The 5th March is the anniversary of her funeral. At that time I was in prison. I learned of her death from the investigator. I used to think that the death of a mother was particularly tragic if there were small children left behind. But now I know that children need their mother at every age.

I have really enjoyed writing to you and have had no problem finding material to write about. But to write to you about my mother is a particularly difficult matter. Why? Firstly, I am aware that no matter how carefully I choose my words I am simply incapable of expressing what I feel towards her and how much I esteemed her. Secondly, she is no longer alive and one should send such thank-you letters to one's mother while she is still alive so that she knows that her life has not been in vain.

The most precious gift a mother could ever have is the gratitude of her children. I know many songs in which love for one's mother is expressed, and very often this love is expressed too late because the mother is no longer alive, and the song-writers lament this in all manner of ways. Yes, human beings never seem to treasure what they actually have.

My beloved mother was a simple Christian. She only attended two classes at church school. She lost her parents at an early age and in 1906 arrived an orphan in Petersburg (now called Leningrad). She then spent her whole life there. That's where she is buried too. It seems to me that her life was filled with all manner of worries.

The evening before my arrest I visited mother without knowing that this was to be the last time that we would see each other. We sat down at the table and talked. She liked to talk and loved to exchange ideas. I asked her, 'Mother, I know that you have gone through a lot, but what do you reckon was the most difficult thing you have experienced in life?' Having asked this question, I prepared myself for her answer, but the answer that came caught me totally off guard. I thought she would say being a widow was hardest, or relate all the terrors of the Leningrad blockade, or the heavy burden of bringing up four small children on her own. But she didn't mention any of this.

Her answer went something like this, 'The difficulties I have experienced in life have all left behind some really joyful memories, because God always helps us in our suffering. The pilgrim who eventually reaches his goal is no longer burdened by memories of the hard times past. Now it is clear to me that I did what the Lord had given me to do. My children are grown up and are all members of the church. The greatest difficulty for me now is waiting for the Lord to take me. Young man, I really want the Lord to come soon and take me.' (She was very seriously ill at that time.)

Seventy-five days after this conversation my mother was in eternity. My sisters explained to me the details of her peaceful, perhaps it would be right to say even joyful, departure to be with the Lord.

The most important thing my mother did for me was to teach me how to pray. Yes, don't be surprised about this. I'll try to explain. I can't remember now the first time I prayed to God, but I can well remember some of the prayers from my earliest childhood.

Our family was poor. But wherever poverty is, God is. In 1941 there was a terrible shortage of food in Leningrad. We were living in a single room of a communal dwelling where other families were living too. A bomb had damaged our house. We had neither light nor heating nor water. The windows were nailed up with plyboard. We thought every day would be our last. People were dying of hunger daily, and as a ten-year-old lad I helped to bury some of them. During those awful days people were not buried in coffins, or even in their own grave. Their corpses were wrapped in sheets and carried into the open air. Then they were all collected by a special lorry and taken to a communal grave.

But God is true in all he says and we experienced his special care. Our family was brought out of Leningrad and saved in an amazing way. How did this happen? I'll tell you briefly.

Mother had taken in a lady with her two small children to live with us in our room. Her house had been burned down after heavy bombing. Ten days later her husband, a colonel, came back from the front to collect her from the city. He was so thankful that we had given his family a place to live that he took us with him in his military vehicle. And so it was that on 14th January 1942 we left Leningrad and travelled thirty five kilometres over the Ladoga Lake. Bombs were falling and the column of vehicles was being fired upon. Vehicles sank beneath the ice and there was death all around us—but God protected us even in these circumstances.

While we were still living in Leningrad, mother would come home very early every morning from her work at the hospital and check if we were still alive. We were all sleeping in one bed under the same blanket to keep warm. One morning at seven o'clock we got out of bed and all knelt down to pray. Mother not only made us pray but would correct our prayers and alter their content. She did this very wisely and with great sensitivity. In the evening she was most regular in leading us in evening prayer.

Have you noticed in the Bible that whenever a king is mentioned his mother is usually mentioned too. The influence of a mother on the development of her child is very, very great. It took me a long while to understand why my childhood memory should be so deeply etched by images of my father. I hardly saw him as he died when I was six years old. I loved to meet people who had known my father well and would always ask them questions. It was only a short while ago that I discovered why I had this deep love for my father.

My mother used to tell us much about father and portray him as an example for us to follow. I learned more about my father from her words than I did about her. Just as a bright light lights up an object, so she illuminated father to us in our consciousness, while she herself remained unnoticed in the shade. This was what my mother, your grandmother Grunya, was like.

Thank God for wise mothers. They are least concerned about themselves. Their whole lives are devoted to their children but rarely do offspring requite this love. Sometimes it can appear to children that their mothers are overly interested and involved in their lives, and their advice and questions seem to be too obtrusive.

I am amazed that such an uneducated woman as my mother knew so many various and complex ways of reaching our hearts. I'll tell you one example.

It was autumn 1942. We had been evacuated from Leningrad to Kirgizia, and we found a temporary home in the house of a single woman. One evening, just after she had retired to her room and before we went to bed, we were praying together.

Before praying in the evening mother would always ask us whether we offended one another in any way, and only when she was sure that everything was straight between us would we pray. That evening she asked us something completely different. 'Children,' she said, 'when you come in the Lord's Prayer to the words "Hallowed be thy name", just pause for a moment and examine your lives. If your behaviour has in any way offended your conscience or someone else's (and thereby the Lord) then don't pray these words. If your conscience does not condemn you, then pray the prayer as normal.'

I thought of all the things we had got up to that day. After saying our own prayers, when it came to praying the Lord's Prayer together I left out those words and remained silent. Everyone went to bed.

Approximately a quarter of an hour later mother called me out into the hallway and asked me, 'Young man, tell me what's up and why you are not happy.' I told mother that I had stolen two tomatoes from a barrel in the cellar belonging to the lady of the house and that I had eaten them (without permission of the owner, of course). Mother got all the details from me and then sent me immediately to the lady of the house so that I could ask her forgiveness. Whatever mother said was law for us, so I went. The lady listened to my apology and came to talk with my mother. Later on I discovered that my confession had pleasantly surprised her and that from then on she allowed my mother to use any of the preserves and pickles as if they were her own.

Thirty-Third Letter

Beloved, in 1 Corinthians 15 the apostle Paul writes the following: 'I die daily.' This is a wonderful portion of Scripture, and in order to understand it you must experience it. Just put yourself in Paul's place: you are brought, not in Soviet handcuffs but in Roman chains, to a four-man body of Jewish scholars. Hundreds of hostile eyes gaze at you, desiring your death. Then the Roman prosecutor reads the charges against you and you are sentenced to death by beheading for having stirred up the people to sedition, and for having lived like a vagrant. The guards leads you to the place of execution, and your parting prayer is upon your lips. You think you spot the eyes of friends and relatives in the crowd. You have commended your spirit to God and the executioner is standing there. Suddenly thunder and lightning breaks out and the storm drives everyone away so that you are brought back into the death cell where you have already perhaps spent several sleepless nights.

So you have another sleepless night. You are emotionally and mentally keyed up, thinking, 'What will the morrow bring?' The next day the same guard, the same Roman soldiers lead you through those same hostile crowds. Once more you receive their scorn, their mocking, their abuse, their malice, their shouting. Again the sentence is read out and again you are brought to the executioner. Then suddenly an armed uprising takes place amongst the people from those that want to keep you from this undeserved execution. Fearing the rebels, the Roman justice commission brings you back into the well-known death cell. The next day is a holiday and no work is being done.

And so the execution is postponed week by week, month by month, but day by day you are experiencing this death. You think that this is to be your last day. Each time you say your farewells to the other prisoners in your cell and each time you bow your knee for the last time in prayer . . . And the days stretch into weeks and the weeks into months.

Now tell me, what do you think would have been easier for the apostle Paul—to die once and for all and to reach his rest, or to taste death day by day, and prepare himself each day to meet Jesus, but then to be brought back to this same cell? Instead of meeting with Jesus he has to go through all of these experiences again and overcome them. For the apostle Paul, and for yourselves too, putting your head on the executioner's block would not be so difficult as the daily experience of the night before, the daily pressure and clanking of the iron chains, the daily starvation, the daily armed guard, the sleeplessness each night. This is what it means by, 'I die daily.' For him, the day of death would have been a day of celebration on which he would go to be with the Lord Jesus, when this daily suffering and dying would have come to an end.

Even though I used to speak to young people about this subject while I was still in freedom, there was no way I could experience the full depth of what Paul meant until I came into a situation like the one I encountered in the prison in Sverdlovsk. That was in 1982. There were approximately fifty of us jammed into a cell for twenty men. There was no question of lying down; there was not even a possibility of sitting down. I squatted on my bag of personal belongings. It was the height of summer. It was clammy in the cell and the sweat just poured off us. There was no ventilation and as soon as everyone began to smoke a dense cloud of smoke enveloped the room. Later on when a match was struck it wouldn't burn because there was no oxygen left. Added to this was the misfortune that above us a sewer pipe had broken and the floor was covered with filth. Exposed to such unhygienic conditions, several criminals developed signs of tuberculosis and were coughing up blood. It was obvious to me that these people with TB were going to die and would never see freedom again. In one or two days' time they would be in their graves. By the following day others had been infected by their sickness and I knew that in one or two days' time I could be among them. Some of them asked a guard to isolate the sick people, but he just looked at us, grinned and said, 'Do you think this is a health resort or something?' Then he closed the small window in the door and went away.

They didn't keep anyone else in these conditions for more than five days, but I was kept in this cell for a good eighteen. But thanks and praise be to God that I escaped death by tuberculosis, even though many others died. There were many other things at that time that made life very difficult but I can't describe them now.

One day a serious criminal was brought into the cell. He was still a young man, about twenty-five years old or so, and he immediately organised a group around him. Sometimes they played cards and told jokes. Suddenly he interrupted them all and turned to me, 'Holy Father, please come here!' I immediately understood that something was going to happen and that if he was calling me over to him then his intentions were not good. I went over to him, maintaining my inner peace, and looked at the group. He asked me, 'Holy Father, go on tell us where you keep your gold.' They all burst out laughing. 'Wherever you work as a priest, you take your wealth with you, don't you? So you've stashed it away somewhere here, if not for yourself, then certainly for your kids. You don't come into prison with nothing.' They were convinced that anyone who worked in a spiritual capacity must also have money.

They used to call me 'Priest'. 'I'm afraid you cannot get my gold, lads,' I answered. They all burst out laughing again. 'Well, we've managed to get plenty of other people's gold!' And he went on to cite all manner of crimes he'd been involved in. One time they had gone to the house of a Jew and demanded his money. When the owner refused to give the money, they took a child, lay it on the table and seared it with a hot iron. He went on to tell of many other sordid and ghastly crimes he had committed. Then he turned to me again, 'So come on, come on tell us where. We will find it.' And I said to them again, 'Lads, you cannot get hold of my riches or my gold, it is in heaven.' And I pointed with my finger to heaven.

Then someone struck a blow into my kidneys from behind and I sank to the floor unconscious. When I came to, I was lying on the bunk. Someone had taken pity on me and laid me there. As soon as I regained my consciousness I sought to reconstruct what had happened. It was hard to get everything clear in my mind, but I was glad that someone had given up their bunk for me. As I was trying to piece things together I suddenly heard the men who the day before had been asking for my gold. One of them said, 'We'll soap down a towel and then hang him with it.' Another voice interrupted, 'Why so much bother, let's just cut his throat with a blade, put it in his hand and say that he committed suicide?' It was very clear to me that they were not just trying to intimidate me, but that they would carry out their threats. I had often witnessed such scenes.

So I briefly prayed for my family, for the church, for the brothers, for the cause of God, and asked him to raise someone up to take my place in the Council of Churches. I also asked the Lord to receive my spirit, and I prepared myself for eternity. And with the heartwarming thoughts of meeting my Lord Jesus Christ, with leaving this place and ascending above the sky to meet my parents in heaven and the martyrs who had gone before there, I fell asleep. The Lord granted me a very peaceful rest. The following day when I went to bed, the same dialogue took place again, 'Come on, we'll hang him. Let's soap down a towel.' 'But why, why don't we just cut his throat?'

Once more I asked the Lord to raise up someone to take my place and prayed for my children that they would be worthy disciples. And I said, 'Lord, if my death will bring more honour to your name than my life, may your will be done.' Again I fell asleep.

Upon waking up I went for a walk outside and as I went down the steps I sang the song, 'Following the bloodstained steps of Christ to my home . . . ' This song was specially meaningful and well known to me. I could well imagine that the composer of this song had also been in a death cell and might have written it before passing over into eternity. As I went down the steps I also thought that my father had been in Sverdlovsk prison at the same age as I, the last but one of the prisons he was to experience. Perhaps he had descended these very same steps . . .

And every day, after the walk, upon returning to the cell, the same thing happened, the same evil intentions to murder me were expressed. This was the first time in my life that I understood what it meant to die daily. I had known about it in my head but had never experienced it until now. Every time I went to bed I was convinced that I would not wake up the next morning and this would be my last night. And when I woke up in the morning I thanked the Lord for another day and I lived this day as if it were my last. For example, many didn't bother to go out for a walk because they couldn't bear the contrast between the fresh air and the stink in the cell. When they got back into the cell they almost passed out. But I always went out in order to breathe my last fresh air and perhaps to hear the twittering of the birds for the last time, or to see the heavens with the white clouds which chased by, for the last time. I knew that any day could be my last.

But the Lord kept me and I remained alive. And when the guard came on the eighteenth day and told us to get ready for transport further, that man who had threatened to cut my throat came over to me, shook my hand and said, 'There's something supernatural about you. This person you call God does exist. Whenever we approached you, you had your eyes closed. But we knew that you heard us. Why didn't you attack us or get hysterical or something? Why didn't you get depressed? Instead you slept so peacefully and serenely. Only someone who really believes in the life to come could do that. When you went out for your walk we thought that you would not return to the cell but would ask one of the guards to put you in another cell. That's what everyone else does. Why did you come back each time? Why did you not ask anyone for help but only prayed to your God every time you got down on your knees by your bunk each evening and each morning? Why did you commit yourself quite calmly into our hands every day? It is simply beyond understanding. You really have got something supernatural about you!' And he shook my hand firmly.

Then he told the other prisoners that they should each contribute something to my journey, so they collected all sorts of food items for me. Between them they filled a net bag with toast, pastry, sugar, dripping—everyone gave whatever he had. So with my little bag of belongings and a big bag full of foodstuffs I boarded the transport wagon. And this food lasted me exactly until Omsk. In truth, we are persecuted but not forsaken. When Elijah went through those most difficult days the Lord sent a raven to feed him. The raven is one of the ugliest of all birds, black and in no way attractive. As the Lord sent a raven to Elijah, so he sent me this violent criminal. He was the blackest of black. But it was he whom the Lord used as a raven to do me good. May the Lord be with you who are in freedom, and may you never forget in your prayers to pray for those who day by day are putting themselves under sentence of death by risking new arrests and new separations. Who do you think finds it harder, myself when I know that on 28th January 1985 I will be released, or those who are living in the underground? Think of Gennadi Konstantinovitch Kryuchkov who has worked for long years under such conditions. Three hundred and sixty-five days in the year for twelve years he has sentenced himself to imprisonment. Also think of many others working under the same conditions but unknown to us. Think of these ones who are sentencing themselves to new arrests and separations, and experience death daily . . .

A Visit to the Penal Camp

Related by Veniamin Mikhailovich Khorev.

I'd like to tell you about a meeting I had with my father
on 7th May 1984. If one were to add together all of his
terms of imprisonment it would mean that we spent
more than ten years 'visiting' father. But this particular
meeting was one of the most unusual, surprising and
beautiful meetings we had. I'll explain later why this
meeting made such an impression upon me.

We reached the penal camp at eleven o'clock on 6th
May, laden with several bags of food. By 'we' I mean my
older brother Vanya who hadn't seen his father since
before his two-year military service, my mother, father's
sister Maria and myself.

So we arrived and went into the reception room where
we filled in the necessary visitors' forms. A young girl of
low rank was sitting at the counter. We had requested a
two-day visit. She looked at the paper and said with
amazement, 'According to my register you are not
booked until 26th May, that is in three weeks' time.'
Now it was our turn to be amazed because we had come
4,000 kilometres, ever since father invited us to come on
this particular date. We immediately went to Lieutenant
Colonel Yegorochkin who is the head of the operations

department, and gave him our form for him to sign. 'We came to visit our father and now we are not being granted the visit,' we said. 'It seems that the date of the visit has been postponed by twenty days. Why? Please would you sign our request?'

'That's not up to me!' he bellowed with his loud, base voice, and thumped the table with his iron fist. 'I didn't grant you a visit!' His eyes began to go bloodshot—he is notorious in the camp for cruelty and malice.

Shortly before our visit I was told of some prisoners from the supervision department who had learned that there was shortly to be a concert in the camp. Upon discovering this one of the prisoners went to Yegorochkin and asked, 'Comrade citizen, wouldn't it be fitting to let us have some hot cabbage soup and an extra ration of vodka as well as allow us to have a bath?' Yegorochkin countered as follows: 'Well, I don't know about hot soup, but I can promise you that you will get fifteen days in solitary confinement for this.' And the prisoner was led away.

We left his office, went down the stairs, and stood at the entrance to the camp, not quite knowing what to do. At that time a jeep passed by and who should get out but Colonel Smolensky, administration head of the corrective labour camp in the Omsk region. All of the officers standing saluted him and everyone else withdrew. Vanya went straight up to him and said gently, 'Leading citizen, we have a request of you.'

'Aha! The Khorevs!' We didn't need to introduce ourselves since he recognised us straight away. Of course, I cannot say that we were the reason he had come, but at least he knew who we were.

Vanya explained to him, 'Leading citizen, we received telegrams and a letter from our father to the effect that our meeting with him was scheduled for the 6th and 7th May. Now we are having difficulties again. Once when we visited he was put in solitary confinement for fifteen days, another time apparently he had violated the clothing regulations and another time there was another reason why we could not meet him. And today we are being told that we can only visit him in twenty days' time. According to their register our visit is booked for 26th May. Leading citizen, if you don't let us meet him this time we will not be able to come on 26th May because we have come from Kishinev which is a very expensive journey of 4,000 kilometres. If we have to turn back now we will go via Moscow and visit the administrative offices there and clarify this matter, which will not be in your interest to do so.'

'Wait a minute, wait a minute,' he said. 'I'll go straight to the camp and ask what's up and why your visit has been refused.' In the meantime, Lieutenant Colonel Yegorochkin had arrived. However, the Chief of the Administration was very polite and kind to us and allowed us to say our piece, which of course did not make the head of the operative department too happy. I'd like to comment again that Smolensky knew all about us, because he didn't have to ask our names. He knew Vanya personally.

Three months previously, after Vanya's demobilisation from the army, he travelled all the way from Tashkent to visit father in this camp, but was only allowed to see him for two or three hours during a general visiting period. He went to Smolensky in the reception room and was told, 'Fill out this form and your visit will be okayed immediately.' Then Smolensky called someone over and during the talk his demeanour changed noticeably, and his face became ashen. Then he said, 'Vanya, if you were to give your father a lecture about atheism I would allow you to meet with him, but I know you certainly won't talk together about anti-religious matters.' So he refused the meeting. Apparently the special department he had phoned up would not give permission for the visit because they were not prepared for it!

I'll explain more about the conversation Smolensky had with father later. Anyway, the next day all four of us were brought into the familiar room where personal visits take place (room number 5) which is situated directly under the office of the operations department. Our meetings always took place in this room. Obviously it was set apart for special people. I was quite amazed that we only had a fleeting and casual search on entering the room. When we left the room only Maria Ivanovna and I were searched. I left the room towards evening because we were not allowed to stay the night. Five officers searched us so thoroughly that they even separated the threads in the handles of our bags.

When father was brought in, Vanya and I met him straight away in the corridor. We greeted him and hugged one another. Mother and Aunty Maria only got to see him as he came into the room. The first thing he said to each of us were these wonderful words, 'Christ is risen!' We all responded in unison each time, 'He is risen indeed!'

From this point in the narrative onwards I would like to speak in father's name because it is much easier for me than to relate what happened during that meeting. It will be nearer to truth and reality.

'I saw you yesterday,' father said. 'I went to the medical department and the windows of this department face out onto "freedom". You were standing right there. I cannot see too well, so I asked one of the prisoners standing near me in the treatment room who was standing outside the visiting-room. "Two women," he said, "a thin one and a larger one, as well as two boys, one of whom is taller than the other." I understood immediately that the thin woman was our Mamochka and the larger woman my sister Maria. The older of the two boys must be Vanya and the younger one Venya (that is, Veniamin). I was so glad to see that you had come to visit me, but I wasn't quite sure how things would go. I didn't understand why things were being delayed, but I had peace just to know that you had come. On the way back to my section I deliberately went via the treatment room so that I could see you again. I also had a good reason: to be checked for lice. Otherwise there is no way they would have allowed me in, because you have to go through numerous inspections to get into the medical department. Back in the section, the Chief of the Administration and Yegorochkin were searching for me.

'Smolensky asked, "Who gave you permission for a visit today. Please will you call the leader of the section?" He was called and Smolensky asked him, "Who authorised the date for this meeting?" The section leader answered, "Oh, the Chief of Staff." "Call in the Chief of Staff, please." So the Chief of Staff was summoned. When they found out from this man who had changed the date of my visit, it turned out that my visiting day had been sold to someone else and that a "2" had been written in front of the "6". And so it turned out that I would have my visit on the 26th. All my superiors had become so corrupt that they thought everything would run smoothly, that my relatives would arrive, see from the schedule that the date had been rescheduled, and then leave nice and peacefully.

'I said, "Leading citizen, I will lodge an official complaint against you if you do not grant my meeting with my family. You know what will happen if the court decides that the meeting was really genuine. I have proof that it was genuine and that someone purely arbitrarily struck the date from the calendar. You know you will lose two months' salary. Now, how much do you earn—300 roubles? Well, you could pay my family your two months' salary to cover their travel costs." He hadn't expected such an onslaught from me, and when he understood what the consequences could be, he said: "Mikhail Ivanovich, don't get so upset. You will have the meeting but first of all I have to ask you something. The letter you sent to your family went through the censorship. But what about your telegrams?" '

Well, father couldn't answer that one because he had had them sent unofficially. But he found a way out of the situation and said, 'Leading citizen, you know that a well-intentioned officer might well have sent those telegrams, or even one of the prisoners no longer under surveillance. There are various ways in which those telegrams could have been sent. Or supposing you, yourself, out of kindness, had decided to do this good deed. Would you want me to betray you?' The officer smiled, stepped to one side, didn't say anything, and left. Father continued, 'Now I can meet you today. How wonderful and inscrutable are the ways of God, and whatever he does is for our best. If we had been granted this meeting yesterday without any complications I would never have been able to speak with so many officers, nor have been able to meet with Smolensky, something I have wanted for a long time. I haven't been able to talk with him for these past four years. But the Lord puts everything together in a wonderful way. To him be the thanks and praise.

'Yesterday an officer came to me and said, "Mikhail Ivanovich, your family's visit has not been granted, and today they have to return home. They said they would not come again on 26th May." By this he wanted either to demoralise me or just inform me, as if I didn't know already. I answered him, "Leading citizen, if they do leave then they will most certainly go via Moscow and that won't be good for you. Secondly, I am happy with what I receive. But I would like to tell you that my God is fulfilling his plans through you and will use you for our blessing. I love my family very much and being together with them means a lot to me, but if it brings more honour to the Lord for us to part rather than be together, then why should I insist on seeing them? If his name is glorified more through my being in prison than through my being at liberty, then I tell you that there is no greater joy for me than to die on this prison bunk as a prisoner, as my father did and as many of my brothers in the faith have done."

'The officer said, "Mikhail Ivanovich, there's so much I don't understand about you." I replied, "There's also so much that I don't understand, but I am not looking for an easy life. And I just cannot comprehend why I have been refused this visit today, but I believe that everything will be revealed in its time." With this we parted.'

At this point father asked us to pray together, and we prayed one after another. I will never forget his prayer because I was listening carefully to what he said, 'My Lord and my God, I bow before you and submit to you, whether in separation from my family, or whether in this present meeting today, for the past and for the present, as well as for the future. I believe that you will give me victory in every new battle I have to go through. And if you are the one who stands at the helm of our lives, you will most certainly steer us safely into the New Jerusalem. Only help us, O Lord, to remain wholeheartedly true to you here on earth, because when we reach eternity there will be no more prisons, deprivations or lawyers or any other way to demonstrate to you our loyalty, because there will be no more fines, or arrests and nothing will separate us from your love. I bow before you, O Lord, in adoration for the fiery chariot that accompanies me everywhere I go, in adoration for the way that I have gone, for the present day, and for future victories. Receive us, O Lord, as your servants, and use

us as your ministers, and love us as your children.
Amen.'

After praying we broke bread together. Then father
continued his thoughts, 'The passage of Scripture in
Isaiah 7:4 (in the Russian Bible) says, "Take heed and
be quiet." What does this mean? It doesn't mean "Be
indifferent towards everything." Not at all. Many would
like to obtain their quietness by non-participation, by
turning away from life and keeping out of all of the
burning issues of the day. They do this just to keep on the
good side of the authorities. Perhaps someone will ask,
"Why complicate one's life by getting involved in such
burning issues?" But our text says, "Take heed." This
means that we should not turn away, but be in the
forefront and in the front line of the battle, together with
God's people. We shouldn't seek an escape out of this
war situation, but march out to meet the enemy—and be
at peace and be quiet. This is much more difficult than
maintaining our peace through non-involvement. So
there are two sorts of people.

'Two painters once agreed that each of them would
paint a picture of "Peace" or "Quietness". After some
time had passed, both presented their pictures. One had
painted a landscape of the Caucasus, with a lake in
which the mountain peaks were reflected. The surface of
the water was quite still, with no breeze; the birds were
flying, the sun was rising and the flowers and trees were
blooming. Around about there was tranquillity and stillness, in one word, "Peace". But I didn't like this picture.

'The other painter painted a large waterfall, the roar-
ing of which could be heard for miles around. There was
turmoil, foam was sprayed around, but above the waterfall there was a tree growing and in the branches of this
tree a bird had made its nest and was feeding its chicks.
This picure also bore the title: "Peace and Quietness".
But this is another sort of peace altogether. This is the

sort of peace that the Lord calls us to. The Lord will lead us to his peace not by an undisturbed life, but by a life which is torn up by turmoil. He does this so that we might trust our God, like those little chicks trusted their mother and didn't have to worry about the warmth or the food she would supply. They needed nothing else, and nothing disturbed them. This shows us how we should "cast all our cares upon the Lord, and the peace of God which passes all understanding will keep our hearts and minds in Christ Jesus."

'For example, yesterday the whole department was alarmed by the appearance of the head of the regional administration. They were all afraid as to what might happen to their visits. No one knew what was up and so everyone was on tenterhooks. Even the leader of the section conveniently disappeared from the camp. Everything was in turmoil around me. Many things were said to me, especially to exercise caution, "Mikhail Ivanovich, don't write anything, and especially don't complain!" In my heart I made no such promises, and had such a peace in the Lord. I had entrusted myself to the Lord, like that little bird, and was at peace.

'In the camp with me was an elder of the church at Ishevsk, a certain Alexei Nikitovich Shubinin, a really good and honest brother. It is really wonderful whenever I meet him and speak with him. We would often think together about the second coming of our Lord. Yesterday he came to me and said, "Mikhail Ivanovich, when I found out that your visit had been cancelled, I got a terrible headache. Why does the Lord seem to bless me so much more than you? I get visitors every four months and they can stay for three days, and yet the one and only visit that you have is cancelled. Let's pray that God will destroy these plans set against you." I replied, "Alexei Nikitovich, I can't pray, nor will I pray like that. I prayed one year ago to see my family, and I won't repeat that prayer. Has he forgotten what I asked for? Or do I have to remind him?" Often we see those things we desire as the most important things there are. Perhaps it would have been better to us, for example, if the writer of Philippians had said, "Let your requests be made known to God and he will fulfill them." But it doesn't say that, it says, "Let your requests be made known to God. And then the peace of God will keep your hearts and minds in Christ Jesus." Whether he fulfils our prayers or not is of no consequence. The main thing is to make requests known to him, and then the peace of God will fill our hearts. And this peace is the greatest compensation for our deprivations.

'On 22nd April we celebrated Easter and this celebration was a very unusual one for me. I got up early on Easter morning, at half past five, which was half an hour before reveille. According to Moscow time it was 2.30 a.m., since we were three hours ahead of Moscow. And I thought of my family and some of the brothers and sisters who would be asleep at this time, or others who would be working the offset machine and printing, and yet others who would be working underground. I brought them all before God in prayer. The events around that first Easter in Christ's life came clearly to mind. In fact, so many thoughts and impressions flooded my mind that were I released at that moment, I would have gone to the nearest church and preached for four or five hours without stopping. I had such a welter of thoughts that came into my mind that I desired eagerly to share them with someone. Then I asked the Lord, "Lord, send me someone I can talk to, that I can talk to about the resurrection and about this day of victory." The Lord, of course, fulfils the desires of the righteous, and at about eight o'clock in the evening, two hours before curfew, an officer came to our barracks and said, "Khorev, over into the staff room!" What does this mean, I thought. Am I going to be transported somewhere else? I knew that none of my superiors would be in the camp at this time. Well, why should I have to go to the staff room then? I was led into a room and the door was locked behind me. There were about fifteen officers sitting around the room. One of them stood up and said, "Mikhail Ivanovich, it's Easter today and we don't know what Easter is all about. Please can you tell us what it's about, if that's possible?"

'I then understood that God was answering the prayer I had offered that morning. I spoke for one and a half to two hours, and it was a wonderful opportunity to speak. No one interrupted me, and everyone listened so attentively that I could have gone on and on speaking. Unfortunately curfew was very near and I had to stop. Could anyone have conceived of organising such a meeting? I had prayed the Lord to send me one of the prisoners to speak to and that Easter Sunday he arranged a proper service for me with fifteen officers present. That's a great miracle. Of course I didn't speak to them in theological jargon, but in simple words. I led them from Golgotha to our present day and then on to the second coming of Christ. I mentioned briefly something about the Old Testament Feast of Passover and then I went on to explain why this festival had come down to us in our generation, and even to this camp, and why I was now amongst these officers speaking about this great Easter Day. Some of the Russian officers there were Jews. To the Russians I spoke Russian, but to the Jews I spoke Yiddish. I said to them that I would be indebted for my whole life to the Jewish people because Christ the Messiah had come from them. The greatest missionary, the apostle Paul, who had devoted his whole life to the preaching of the gospel, and mostly to Gentiles, and by preaching to Gentiles had also indirectly evangelised our country and caused me and my family to come to know Christ. And he was also a Jew. All the apostles were Jews and the Jewish people have always been and always will be the index finger of God in world history. And God would allow the whole process to continue until people like myself, the Gentiles, completed the full number of saved sinners. Then the Lord would receive the Jews back to himself. Everyone listened, of course, with rapt attention. The mention of the Jewish people really fell on good ground in the hearts of these Jewish officers and the next day I noticed a distinctly more friendly attitude towards me.

'As for Easter Sunday, I would like to go back again to that morning prayer I uttered. I decided to greet the first person that I met with the words, "Christ is risen." The first prisoner that I met just stared at me and asked, "Have you gone crazy?" I decided that if he thought I was crazy the best thing for me to do was not to begin talking to him but rather go on to greet the next one. I went on my way and another prisoner summoned me, "Mikhail Ivanovich, I have got something to talk to you about." "Well," I thought, "what does he want from me?" I had never had anything to do with him. He whispered in my ear, "Christ is risen!" Now since he whispered it to me I replied to him softly, "He is risen indeed!" Why should you embarrass someone if he doesn't want to share this festival of the resurrection with anyone else? I went on into the section and there were twenty prisoners sitting there. Suddenly a prisoner came running into the room and shouted, "Comrades, our Jesus is risen!" Then he added, "We must celebrate this, either with cognac or with chifir!" Everyone waited to hear what I would say. All I did was calmly take three eggs, unpainted of course—don't ask me where I got them from, otherwise the operative department will be on my back—I'll tell you once I am free! So I took these three eggs, shelled them, divided them into twenty portions and gave a piece to each of the prisoners and replied to them all, "He is risen indeed!" This was, of course, very unusual behaviour, and no one had expected such a response from me.

'During the day, right up until evening, I had the most varied responses to that Easter greeting of mine: "Christ is risen!" Many answered purely as a matter of form, simply by way of reply. It was only towards evening that I met Alexei Nikitovich. I greeted him, "Christ is risen!" And he greeted me equally as loudly and triumphantly: "He is risen indeed!" We hugged one another as close brothers and wished each other well. We held one another for several minutes. None of the criminals could understand the warmth of our greeting, because they had no part in Christ. So during that day one person had thought I was mad, another had whispered the greeting in my ear, others had greeted me purely formally, with no feeling but simply by way of reply . . .

'When we greet one another on this Easter Sunday in this way, "Christ is risen!", then it is not only important that we answer, but it is also vital how we answer. If Christ is indeed risen in our hearts this will be a festival that goes on our whole life long, a never-ending festival. For me it is the greatest of all festivals. On this day of victory we should shout out triumphantly, "Hurrah! Christ is risen indeed!" And when I regain my freedom, should the Lord allow it, then wherever I am on 28th January I will greet everyone in all the churches, even though it be in the middle of the winter, with these words, "Christ is risen indeed!", and I won't do that just because it's nice or a new thing to do, or to make something of myself, but simply because it is the greatest festival in my whole life.

'Or, what do you make of the passage in 1 Corinthians 15:29–31, "Now if there is no resurrection, what will those do who are baptised for the dead? If the dead are not raised at all why are people baptised for them? And

as for us, why do we endanger ourselves every hour?"
The apostle Paul wrote to the church in Corinth, " . . . I
die daily." Baptism is, above all, an immersion. Before it
takes place three conditions must be met: there must be a
place for the immersion, an immerser and a person to be
immersed. According to this text the place of immersion
was the daily needs, sufferings and persecutions by
which the writer experienced death daily. The baptiser
was the Lord, and the person to be baptised was the
apostle Paul. In other words, he was saying if we are not
to be raised, if those to whom I preach are not to be
raised, why am I daily immersed in these needs, suffering
scorn, hunger and cold, never eating enough and continually being surrounded by danger and torment, languishing in prisons, perhaps in the oppressive
subterranean vaults of Rome? The apostle is questioning
whether we would bear the cost of all this for the sake of
men who would never be raised again. But if the resurrection really took place, if we will live for ever and be
with our resurrected Lord for ever, then I am not dying
in vain and it is worthwhile going this way, and fighting
and giving one's whole life. It is worthwhile living under
such daily pressures for the sake of preaching the gospel.

'If there is a resurrection then it is not in vain that I
have been on trial. Nor was it in vain that I was in
Sverdlovsk prison where I died "daily". Nor was it in
vain that I made that exhausting and dangerous journey
transported from Kishinev to Odessa, Kharkov, Rostov,
Sverdlovsk and finally to Omsk. Because when I reach
heaven I will receive the reward for having gone this
way.

'That's the reason why this greeting "He is risen
indeed!" is so important and so deeply moving. It has to
do with life or death. Is he risen or is he not risen? So,
beloved, let me greet you and point you to that glorious
and eternal festival of the resurrection of Christ. I do this

with a heart that is deeply moved. But only those should reply "He is risen indeed" in whose hearts Christ has really been risen. Only those who are convinced that the way of imprisonment and suffering our Christian brothers and myself are taking is not in vain but is the right way to go. And so let us say, "Christ is risen!".'

And we all answered in unison, 'He is risen indeed!'

This visit was rich and full of spiritual nourishment for us. For this reason it was one of the most unusual times that we had ever spent with father. Afterwards I said to him, 'We are the ones who have friends, literature and information, we are the ones who have fellowship and conversation and really it should be us who are communicating life to you. But I have to confess that when we come to visit you we just have to remain silent. We have nothing to say but we listen to you because you communicate this life to us.' And really that was the way it was, as he himself said, 'I am in a gold mine and am mining gold which is purified in the fire.' And father gave us some of those nuggets of gold during that visit we made to him.

Just a few words about the situation in which father later found himself. In February a KGB worker from Moldavia visited him and spoke with him, or to be more exact, gave him a verbal working over for two days. He was especially interested in father's behaviour, 'What will you do when you are released?' Father answered that he was not accustomed to, nor did he have the intention of, talking with the KGB about what he would do when he was released. Basically they wanted to know whether he would have the churches in Moldavia registered after his release. Father gave him no answer, but he only said, 'Please excuse me, but it is still several months before my release, and who knows what sort of revolutions could take place in the Kremlin in the meantime, even with regard to the 1929 legislation governing religious cults? So I really cannot tell you what I think of registration. Let's wait until I am released and then we will see.'

It's known to us that the editions of *Vestnik Istiny* containing these letters entitled 'I write to you, children' are being stored in the special department of the KGB. 'Of course,' said Father, 'they are not talking about a new case against me yet, but I am aware that they are keeping a special watch on me. I know that every word I whisper to a prisoner is monitored in the operations department and I am being watched in a special way as never before. For example, recently I was searched, and not only was every piece of empty writing paper confiscated but also a few sweet wrappings too. They are literally taking everything away from me. At first I didn't understand why, but now I do.'

But when we told him that his letters are being read throughout the whole world and even translated into other languages, he was amazed and very happy. He said, 'I am prepared to go to prison for another five years for those letters, just so that God's people might know the truth about our life, not only about my life but about the life of all prisoners for Christ. But I believe that the Lord will grant me a time to be together with my friends. I know that many are waiting for me, co-workers, churches, family, and brothers in the leadership. Let us kneel down before the Lord and say, "Thy will be done." Whatever happens, let us always be ready to thank the Lord for it.'

In a conversation he once had with his family, Mikhail Khorev made the following remark, 'I ask you not to despair if you discover that they have pinned a second term of imprisonment on me. Don't feel that you are orphans or a widow. But when you discover this, kneel down and thank the Lord for his way which is incomprehensible to us here on earth. One day in heaven it will become comprehensible. So thank him that he is our Lord and God and this is the greatest thing we know, and thus he deserves all our thanks and worship in all the circumstances that we might find ourselves in in life.'

In November 1984 Mikhail Ivanovich Khorev was sentenced to a further two years in the strict regime penal camp in Omsk.

He was released at the end of his term in December 1986, and returned to his home town, Kishinev. Not long afterwards, he left home again, in order to continue his itinerant preaching ministry, now underground, advising pastors and evangelising within the independent evangelical churches in the USSR. Mikhail's sons, Pavel, Veniamin and Ivan are assuming leadership roles within the youth groups and churches, and Veniamin was arrested once himself . . .

Notes

1   KGB (Komitet gossudarstvenoy bezopasnosti), literally translated, means, 'Committee for State Security'.
This is the Soviet secret service.

2   Georgi Petrovich Vins (born 1928) from Kiev, was
elected secretary of the Council of Churches of the Evangelical Christian Baptists (CCECB). This Council was
established in 1965. Since his deportation from the
USSR in April 1979 (after a five-year term of imprisonment) he has been living with his family in Elkhart,
USA, where he was commissioned by the Council of the
Churches to set up a foreign office for the ECB. In
Russian, people are usually referred to by their first
name and patronymic (ie father's personal name)—eg
Georgi Petrovich, Mikhail Ivanovich.

3   The 'legislation governing religious cults' refers to
the injunction 'about religious assembly', which came
into force on 8th April 1929. This downgrades the practice of religion to 'the satisfaction of the most basic
religious needs'. Any religious assembly has to be 'registered' and therefore subject itself to extremely limiting
conditions. Even today the recognition of this law is a
prerequisite for 'legalising' or registering any Christian
fellowship.

4   The Union of Evangelical Christian Baptists (ECB) was founded towards the end of October 1944, after pressure was brought to bear by the Soviet authorities. It was made up of two streams of free churches: one stream calling themselves the Evangelical Christians and the other stream calling themselves Baptists. In 1946 the 'Christians of the Evangelical Faith' (Pentecostals) were added, followed by the 'Christians of the Evangelical Faith in the Spirit of the Apostles' (Apostolics) in 1947. Then in 1961 a part of the Mennonite Brethren Churches joined.

In 1961 part of the ECB separated from the main body of the Union because it felt that it could no longer allow itself to be dictated to by the atheistic state. In 1965 they formed their own union, which was led by the Council of the Churches (see notes 2 above and 8 below), and this has not been recognised by the state. Neither Pentecostals nor 'Apostolic Christians' belong to it.

5   The decree which separated church and state, and school from church came into force on 23rd January 1918. According to this law, all citizens are granted the same civil rights regardless of their religious viewpoint. Strictly speaking, because of this decree there should be no mention of belonging or not belonging to a religious persuasion on any official documentation. Any influence this decree might have had was negated by later decrees, injunctions and amendments, so that today it is purely a showpiece decree.

6   The 'All Union Council' acts as the leader of the Council of ECB churches (hence AUCECB). It is a member of the World Council of Churches and of the Christian Peace Conference.

7   'The Messenger of Truth' (in Russian *Vestnik Istiny*). This periodical of the unregistered Evangelical Christian Baptists is issued four times a year by the secret printing press, 'Khristianin', and it contains news from the

various churches as well as reflections on spiritual matters.

8　Gennadi Konstantinovich Kryuchkov (born 1928), from Tula, has been president of the Council of Unregistered ECB Churches since 1965, (see point 4). Since 1971 he has been living underground and the authorities are presently searching for him.

9　Pavel Frolovich Sakharov (1922–71) was a gifted evangelist, poet and composer. He was imprisoned several times because of his faith. His health suffered severely in prison. Sakharov occupied an important position in the Union of non-registered ECB Churches.

10　'Roasting' prisoners' clothing. This was a measure that was taken to destroy any lice in prisoners' clothing. To do this, the personal effects of prisoners were heated in special rooms to very high temperatures, usually while the prisoners were taking showers. The 'roasting' of the clothing doesn't only occur when there is an outbreak of lice but very often whenever a prisoner arrives at a new prison camp.

11　Pyotr Danilovich Peters (born 1942) since his youth has been one of those persecuted for his faith. At the age of sixteen he was literally chased out of his village. Since then he has not really been able to reside anywhere for long. He has either been in prison (at the time of writing he is serving a five-year term of imprisonment) or he has lived underground. Only after being released from prison was he able to return for a short time to a 'legal' lifestyle. He is a member of the Council of the Churches.

12　Initiativniki—a group of brothers who led the split from the official Baptist Union in 1961.

More information about the independent evangelical churches in the Soviet Union is available free of charge from Friedensstimme (UK) (a mission which represents, aids and defends the interests of the CCECB in close co-operation with Georgi Vins).

Friedensstimme (UK)
PO Box 10
Leicester
LE3 2FX

Tel (0455) 633856